Workshop Models for Family Life Education

Adult Children
of Alcoholics

Workshop Models for Family Life Education

Adult Children of Alcoholics

Phyllis Tainey

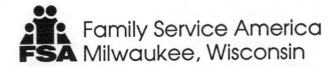

Family Service America
Milwaukee, Wisconsin

Copyright (c) 1988
Family Service America
11700 West Lake Park Drive
Milwaukee, Wisconsin 53224

Library of Congress Cataloging-in-Publication Data

Tainey, Phyllis
   Adult children of alcoholics / Phyllis Tainey.
      p.   cm. — (Workshop models for family life education)
   Includes bibliographies.
   ISBN 0-87304-222-0
   1. Adult children of alcoholics—Counseling of—United States.
   2. Social group work—United States. I. Title. II. Series.
   HV5132.T35 1988
   362.2'92—dc19

                                          88-24398
                                            CIP

TABLE OF CONTENTS

85929

PREFACE

Workshop Models for Family Life Education is a series of manuals intended to promote the exploration of new alternatives and the utilization of new options in day-to-day living through programs in family life education.

Basically, family life education (FLE) is a service of planned intervention that applies the dynamic process of group learning to improving the quality of individual and family living. The manuals are in workshop format and offer new approaches to service to families. They are meant to serve as a training mechanism and basic framework for group leaders involved in FLE workshops.

In 1974, the Family Service Association of America (FSAA), now Family Service America, appointed a National Task Force on Family Life Education, Development, and Enrichment. One of the goals of the task force was to assess the importance and future direction of FLE services within family service agencies. One of the recommendations of its report was to "recognize family life education, development, and enrichment as one of the three major services of the family service agency: family counseling, family life education, and family advocacy."[1] This recommendation was adopted by the association's Board of Directors and has become basic policy.

An interest in FLE is a natural development of Family Service America's role in the strengthening of family life and complementary to the more traditional remedial functions of family agencies. Family Life Education programs can add a new dimension to the services provided by family agencies. They can open an agency to the general population by providing programs that are appropriate for all families and individuals, not only for those at risk. They provide a new arena for service that deals with growth as well as dysfunction. They can encourage agencies to look beyond the therapeutic approach and to take on a new objective for the enrichment and strengthening of family life. For the participants, FLE programs can lead to increased understanding of normal stress, growth of esteem for one's self and others, development of communications skills, improved ability to cope with problem situations, development of problem-solving skills, and maximization of family and individual potential.

This series provides tangible evidence of Family Service America's continuing interest in FLE and of a belief in its future importance for family services. Family Life Education programs, coordinated within a total agency program and viewed as a vital and integral part of the agency, can become key factors in promoting growth and development within all families.

1. "Overview of Findings of the FSAA Task Force on Family Life Education, Development, and Enrichment," mimeographed (New York: Family Service Association of America, May 1976), p. 21.

ACKNOWLEDGMENTS

The information contained in the mini-lectures throughout the text draws largely from the works of Claudia Black, Ph.D., and Janet Geringer Woititz, Ed.D., both of whom have written extensively on adult children of alcoholics. I would like to thank them for the tremendous contribution they have made to the growing body of knowledge about adult children of alcoholics and for their excellent books, which have made it possible to share this knowledge with both professionals and laypersons alike. I also thank them for their kind permission to use their material extensively. Much of the material in the present workbook is taken directly from Black's book, *It Will Never Happen to Me!*, as well as from her lectures and seminars (quotes from these lectures are cited as "from the works of Claudia Black" and are referred to throughout the manual by an asterisk), and from Woititz's *Adult Children of Alcoholics*.[1] Without their contribution to the literature, this workshop model would not exist. I would also like to thank John Horsey, Regional Services Representative of Spofford Hall, New Hampshire, for inviting me to attend a seminar given by Claudia Black at his facility in the spring of 1983. It was there that I first heard the words "adult children of alcoholics." Exposure to this body of knowledge has had a tremendous impact on my ability to help clients, so many of whom are adult children of alcoholics. I would also like to thank John Horsey for his continued encouragement and support in the writing of this program. I am grateful to Margaret G. Sumner, Coordinator of the Family Life Enrichment Program at Child and Family Services, Hartford, Connecticut, for all that I have learned from her over the years and for her continued interest and assistance in helping to create this program.

Phyllis Tainey

1. Claudia Black, *It Will Never Happen to Me!* (Denver: ACT, 1981); Janet Geringer Woititz, *Adult Children of Alcoholics* (Pompano Beach, Fla.: Health Communications, 1983).

INTRODUCTION

The Family Life Enrichment Program at Child and Family Services of Hartford, Connecticut, has developed a variety of workshop models to address client needs, including two workshop models that relate specifically to the effects of alcoholism on the individual and the family. The first of these workshops, "The Road to Alcoholism, Facts and Fiction," by Phyllis Tainey and Margaret G. Sumner, was designed for individuals who wish to increase their knowledge and awareness of alcoholism as a disease. This model was aimed toward those who might be concerned about their own drinking or the drinking of a family member, employee, or friend.

The creation of a program designed specifically for adult children of alcoholics grew out of the increasing awareness over the past few years that individuals who have grown up in alcoholic families continue to be affected by this experience in their adulthood. As a result of living with parental alcoholism, adult children of alcoholics must deal with issues concerning trust; appropriate expression of anger; inability to feel or express their feelings; difficulty with intimate relationships; low self-esteem; a sense of emptiness and depression; and tendencies toward workaholism, chemical dependency, or other compulsive behaviors.

Therefore, the objectives of the present workshop are to provide a structured, supportive group environment in which individuals are able to understand these issues and discuss the impact of their childhood experiences on their adult lives and to help them become aware of the connection between their past experiences and present behavior. The workshop examines in detail what it is like to grow up in an alcoholic family; the rules of the home, such as "Don't Talk, Don't Feel, Don't Trust"; the roles in the home that get carried into adulthood; issues specific to adult children of alcoholics; and the importance of self-help and therapy groups as a vital part of the recovery process.

One of the goals of this workshop is to dispel the sense of isolation and "being different" that adult children of alcoholics so often experience and to begin the reversal of the rules that govern the alcoholic home. This goal is achieved through the sharing of individual experiences and feelings, which in turn allows members to identify and relate with each other. It is important for leaders to create an atmosphere of validation and support. Mini-lectures help members achieve this sense of validation and increased self-understanding by providing information that supports their experiences.

General Information

This structured and time-limited workshop model consists of eight two-hour sessions. The workshop is most effective when membership is limited to fifteen participants. Smaller groups, of ten to twelve people, allow more time for individual sharing and group discussion. The model uses mini-lectures to provide didactic information to group members, exercises to be done in small groups, and full-group discussions to provide an experiential component.

The program is designed to produce a balance between increased intellectual and emotional awareness for participants. Although experiencing feelings is encouraged, and must be handled with extreme sensitivity on the part of the group leader through support and validation, the workshop is not intended to be a therapy or treatment group per se. The structure of the workshop, as well as its emphasis on education, tends to increase the comfort level of individuals who have learned not to feel in order to survive the emotional trauma of their past.

In order to empathize and validate, group leaders must have an in-depth understanding of adult children of alcoholics and the issues that they face as well as a basic knowledge and understanding of alcoholism as a family disease. Leaders must be prepared to answer questions related to alcoholism and its effect on the individual and the family. They should also be prepared to admit their lack of knowledge if they do not know the answer to a question, and demonstrate a willingness to find the answer.

Group leaders must read extensively on adult children of alcoholics. Two very helpful books for group leaders and group members alike are *It Will Never Happen to Me!* by Claudia Black and *Adult Children of Alcoholics* by Janet Geringer Woititz. Other helpful books for group members are Black's *Repeat After Me*, Woititz's *Struggle for Intimacy*, and Charles Deutsch's *Broken Bottles, Broken Dreams*.[1]

Leaders should know and understand the material in each session. They should be thoroughly familiar with the manual before beginning the workshop and should review the outline and material for each session before it is presented. As much as possible, the material should be discussed with group members and not just read or lectured to them. Eye contact is important.

2

It is helpful to prepare for sessions in advance by arranging chairs in a circle and listing exercise questions on a flip chart before members come in. Flip charts are important teaching tools; they help clients learn visually as well as through their auditory senses. Writing questions on the flip chart and listing members' responses below the question is an effective way to empha- size and reinforce important points.

It is helpful if leaders have had previous experience leading Family Life Education groups and have a basic understanding of how the model works. Group-work skills, such as relating a point made by one member with a pre- vious comment made by another member, are helpful. The leader should reinforce members' contributions by saying "I'm glad you brought that up," "Good point!" or "Thank you for sharing that."

Because the workshop was designed so that the information that is present- ed and the themes and issues that are developed have continuity from one session to another, sessions should be presented in the order that is suggest- ed. A lot of material must be covered in each session. As members begin to feel comfortable with the workshop and discussion increases, leaders may find it difficult at times to cover the session content in depth. With a large group or when the participation level is high, the leader may find it useful to incorporate the content of the mini-lectures into the group discussion at the end of an exercise. The workshop can easily be stretched into ten sessions if the leader wants to allow more time for sharing and group discussion. Although group members may be reluctant to share when the workshop begins, the supportive nature of the group eventually leads members to express painful experiences and emotions such as intense sadness, anger, grief, or fear. Leaders must be prepared to validate and support these feel- ings and to demonstrate sensitivity in their responses. Leaders should be concerned, confident, committed, and empathic.

Although the curriculum is highly stuctured, its primary purpose is to guide learning. Changes can be made in the basic curriculum to meet the style of the leader or the needs of the group.

---

1. Claudia Black, *It Will Never Happen to Me!*; Janet Geringer Woititz, *Adult Children of Alcoholics*; Claudia Black, *Repeat after Me* (Denver: ACT, 1985); Janet Geringer Woititz, *Struggle for Intimacy* (Pompano Beach, Fla.: Health Communications, 1985); and Charles Deutsch, *Broken Bottles, Broken Dreams* (New York: Teachers College Press, 1982).

PREPARATION FOR THE WORKSHOP

Recruiting for the Group

Combining several approaches should result in successful recruiting for the workshop.

For group leaders who are associated with or in practice at a family service agency, mental health clinic, or other treatment facility, recruitment can begin with one's own clients. Clients should be made aware of the benefits of the group experience and told that it is designed to address their specific needs and issues. Leaders should educate and inform other agency staff about whom the workshop would benefit so that appropriate client referrals can be made.

Public service radio announcements, either thirty or sixty seconds long, help generate inquiries and client registration. For example,

> If you grew up in an alcoholic home, you are probably still being affected by this experience as an adult. Adult children of alcoholics feel isolated from other people and have difficulty with trust and communication of feelings. They suffer from low self-esteem, fear of abandonment and rejection, problems with close relationships, fear of angry people, and a strong need for approval from others. Individuals with these concerns often benefit from sharing their problems in a group. If you are concerned with these issues, _____ (name of agency or organization) has a workshop for you called Adult Children of Alcoholics. For more information or to register call _____ (agency phone number), that's _____ (repeat number).

Newspapers will also run a feature article on a workshop or announce the starting date of the program under their listing of community events.

Registration

Registration can begin on the telephone. When potential clients call to inquire about the group, they should be told that the workshop is not a therapy group or self-help program but an adult education workshop with an experiential component. The leader should give a broad overview of the content of each session, as well as information about the time, dates, and fee for the workshop. Some individuals may be hesitant to commit for the full eight weeks because of their anxiety about addressing their issues as an adult child. However, potential registrants should be told that they should register only if they are willing to make a commitment for a full eight weeks' attendance, barring illness or unforeseen events. Members should be told to arrive fifteen to twenty minutes before the first group meeting to pay the registration fee for the workshop and to complete paperwork.

The use of name tags is a good idea for at least the first few group sessions and may facilitate sharing in small groups. Groups should meet in a room that comfortably accommodates the size of the group. Chairs should be placed in an open circle, with the leader's chair and flip chart at the open end.

SESSION 1

OBJECTIVES: To provide information on statistics concerning adult children of alcoholics.
To discuss how the child is affected by the alcoholic parent's behavior.
To increase awareness of parental inconsistency and rigidity.
To increase awareness of the effects of the nonalcoholic parent.
To discuss issues of self-esteem and lack of resources for children of alcoholics.

I. INTRODUCTION

A. As members enter room, give them outline and bibliography (see Session 1 handouts).

B. *Leader Introduces Self*
When all group members have arrived, the leader introduces self to the group, giving name, position or title, and any other appropriate identifying information. The leader may share information about his or her professional background to facilitate group confidence.

C. *Introduction of Members*
Ask group members to introduce themselves to the group by stating their first names.

D. *Purpose of Workshop*
The group leader may wish to state the following:

You are here because you are interested in learning more about how growing up in an alcoholic family system has affected you as a child and how it continues to affect you as an adult. You may be here because you were a child in an alcoholic family and are now interested in learning more about the issues concerning adult children of alcoholics and how they affect your life. This group's purpose is to discuss the problems that arise from growing up in an alcoholic home and to increase your awareness of how these problems continue to affect you in your adult life. An alcoholic home or family is a home or family in which one or more members has been affected by the disease of alcoholism, be it their own alcoholism or that of their parents or grandparents. The terms adult children and adult child refer to adult individuals who at one time were children in an alcoholic family, not to the emotional maturity of these individuals.

As adult children of alcoholics, you suffer from the "disease" of codependency. Like alcoholism, the disease of codependency is emotional, physical, and spiritual in nature. It is a condition that develops in dysfunctional families that are rigid, critical, negative, perfectionistic, and repressive in nature, and in which feelings are not allowed to be talked about openly. Usually these families have secrets, such as alcoholism, mental illness, incest, physical or emotional abuse, that are not talked about and that are dealt with through denial.

Children in a codependent family learn to deny their true self, who they really are, in a futile attempt to win their parents' love and approval, which is always conditional in nature, or these children repeatedly learn to repress and deny their true self and instead develop a false or codependent self. Consequently, these children become disconnected from who they really are. Codependency causes children to become overly dependent on others for their sense of self-esteem and nurturing, even into adulthood, because their dependency needs were not sufficiently met in childhood. Codependents may develop stress-related illnesses from repressing their feelings, such as migraines, intestinal disorders, cancer, heart problems, and high blood pressure. Like alcoholism, codependency is a family disease that is passed from one generation to the next. To recover from codependency, individuals must also become involved in a twelve-step recovery program and treatment. One cannot recover from this disease alone or in isolation, because isolating oneself in one's pain is a major component of this disease.

This group is not a treatment or therapy group. However, we will provide resources for support groups, treatment, and recovery programs at the end of the workshop.

E. *Overview of Format and Content*
This workshop is a structured, time-limited series that meets eight times. Meetings are two hours long and begin promptly. If you cannot attend a session, please let me know.

We will use mini-lectures to provide you with information. We will ask you to work in small groups before holding full-group discussions so that you can draw on personal experiences more easily.

Please share only as much as you feel comfortable sharing. You do not have to share any more than you want. We find that those who share get the most out of the group. I realize that some of these topics may be painful or difficult to discuss, especially for adult children of alcoholics. However, as you learn more about the connection between your past and your present, it will become easier for you to accept yourself and your feelings.

There is a lot of material to cover in eight sessions, so sometimes we may have to move on to the next topic without discussing a topic as thoroughly as we might like.

Confidentiality is an important issue. That which is discussed in the group must stay in the group. People may not want to be recognized outside the group. Therefore, we request that members respect the confidentiality of others.

II. SHARING EXPECTATIONS OF GROUP MEMBERS: EXERCISE ONE

A. Objective: To provide members with an opportunity to express what they would like to learn from the group.

B. Ask members to pair up with someone whom they do not know.

C. Request that they share with their partner what it is they hope to get from the group.

D. Debrief: Members gather to discuss the same question as a group.

E. List responses on flip chart. Use for review at end of group exercise.

III. MINI-LECTURE: WHY ARE WE INTERESTED IN LEARNING MORE ABOUT ADULT CHILDREN OF ALCOHOLICS?

A. The following quotes are taken from the Charter Statement of the National Association for Children of Alcoholics and from other sources as noted.
   1. "An estimated 28 million Americans have at least one alcoholic

parent. Of these, about 15 million are school children, 13 million are adults."

2. "More than half of all alcoholics have an alcoholic parent."

3. "One out of every three families reports alcohol abuse by a family member."

4. "Children of alcoholics are at the highest risk of developing alcoholism themselves or marrying someone who becomes an alcoholic."

5. "Medical research has shown that children born to alcoholics are at the highest risk of developing attention deficit disorders, stress-related medical problems, fetal alcohol syndrome, and other alcohol-related birth defects."

6. "In up to 90 percent of child abuse cases, alcohol is a significant factor."

7. "Children of alcoholics are also frequently victims of incest, neglect and other forms of violence and exploitation." There is a high incidence of alcoholism among incestuous fathers. Because victims of physical and sexual abuse tend to be abusive to their own children, family alcoholism may result not only in victims but in perpetrators of abuse.[1]

8. Parental alcoholism often results in emotional problems. In one study, mental illness was diagnosed twice as often in children of alcoholics than it was in children of schizophrenics.[2] The psychological problems associated with parental alcoholism are chronic depression, psychosomatic complaints, social aggression, emotional detachment and isolation, attempted and completed suicides, learning disabilities, anxiety, eating disorders, and compulsive achieving. Children of alcoholics often live through divorce, placements in foster care, or have delinquent reactions.[3]

9. Children of alcoholics often adapt to the chaos and inconsistency in the alcoholic home by developing an inability to trust, an extreme need to control, and by learning to deny and not discuss their feelings or needs. They learn the rules of the home, "don't talk, don't feel, don't trust."[4] This results in low self-esteem and difficulty in developing necessary social skills. Adult children find it difficult to maintain satisfying or intimate personal relationships, which leaves them feeling depressed, isolated, guilty, or fearful. Some adult children develop an excessive sense of responsibility, which results in their becoming rigid and controlling. Some become overly dependent on others and feel no sense of power or choice.

10. "The problems of most children of alcoholics remain invisible, because their coping behavior tends to be approval seeking, peo-

ple pleasing, and socially acceptable. However, a disproportionate number of those entering the juvenile justice system, courts and prisons, mental health facilities, and those referred to school authorities are children of alcoholics."

11. "The majority of people served by employee assistance programs are adult children of alcoholics."

Claudia Black states that children who grow up in an alcoholic home have fewer resources than do children from homes in which alcoholism is not a problem. They may have fewer physical resources because they are kept awake at night by their parents' fighting, which drains them physically and emotionally and may interfere with their ability to concentrate on school work. They may also have fewer resources because of physical or sexual abuse. In up to 90 percent of child abuse cases, alcohol is a significant factor. Worrying about the next time he or she will be abused also hinders the child's ability to concentrate at school. The child fears the parents' drinking and worries about the family.

The child has fewer emotional resources because he or she is anxious about the alcoholic's behavior and is affected by the anxiety of the nonalcoholic spouse. The child may be asked to take sides or report on the alcoholic's drinking, which results in feelings of disloyalty.

Socially, children of alcoholics have fewer resources. They do not feel free to discuss their problems outside the home because doing so leaves them with a sense of betrayal. They are told by the parents not to let anyone outside the home know what is going on in the home. Like the alcoholic and the nonalcoholic spouse, they try to hide the problem from the world. They may feel ashamed of the drinking and may be afraid to bring friends home because they are afraid of being embarrassed by their parents' alcoholic behavior.

The child in an alcoholic home also has fewer resources socially because he or she has difficulty connecting with others. Children in an alcoholic home do not learn to talk honestly about their feelings.*

Ask group members if they have any questions about the preceding material.

---

*Material referred to here and throughout the text by an asterisk is drawn from lectures and seminars presented by Claudia Black.

IV. HOW THE CHILD IS AFFECTED BY THE BEHAVIOR OF THE ALCOHOLIC AND THE NONALCOHOLIC PARENT

A. *Exercise Two*
   1. Objective: To increase members' awareness of how the alcoholic and nonalcoholic parents' behavior affected them when they were children.
   2. Break into dyads.
   3. Ask members the following questions:
      - How were you affected as a child by the alcoholic's behavior as a parent?
      - How were you affected as a child by the behavior of the non-alcoholic parent?
   4. Discuss the first question. The following points should be included:
      - As a child you did not receive consistent discipline, setting of limits, or parenting.
      - Your parents could be loving one minute and rejecting the next.
      - Your parents were overly strict one minute and overly lenient the next.
      - There was a vast discrepancy between sober and drunk behavior, which resulted in your not knowing what to expect from the alcoholic parent.
      - You did not receive consistent nurturing or loving behavior from the alcoholic, which affected your ability to trust.
      - The alcoholic parent made promises and broke them, thus affecting your ability to develop trust in others and your ability to depend on people to do what they said they would do.
      - This experience caused problems in developing closeness, intimacy, and trust later in life.
      - You may have been physically and emotionally neglected by the alcoholic parent (perhaps because he or she was sleeping off a hangover).
      - You may have had to assume the role of parent.
      - You may have had to take care of yourself, your parents, or your younger siblings.
      - Your own dependency needs were not met.
      - You felt insecure attempting to perform adult tasks without adult skills.
      - You became preoccupied with worrying about the alcoholic's drinking.
      - Your parents were very rigid. They were always right. You either did things their way or the wrong way. Everything

12

was black or white, right or wrong, good or bad. The alcoholic could become very angry when you wanted to do things your own way. Consequently, you would do anything to avoid disapproval, anger, or conflict or to gain the alcoholic's approval. Because you always tried to please your parents, you lost your own identity. No emphasis was placed on your needs or wishes. This behavior occurred with the nonalcoholic parent as well, who could be equally rigid and controlling.

5. Discuss the second question. Include the following points:
   - Your nonalcoholic parent was preoccupied with the alcoholic and his or her drinking.
   - As the disease progressed, the nonalcoholic parent became less available to you emotionally, as did the alcoholic parent, eventually becoming depressed.
   - The nonalcoholic parent may have taken his or her frustrations out on you or appeared irritable.
   - You may have felt ignored or unloved.
   - The nonalcoholic parent failed to protect you from the abuse, neglect, or inconsistency of the alcoholic parent by not setting limits on the unacceptable behavior and by choosing to remain with the alcoholic in order to meet his or her own dependency needs. Consequently, you did not grow up in an emotionally secure environment.
   - You may have seen the nonalcoholic parent as overburdened. You were reluctant to go to this parent with your problems.
   - You did not receive enough focused attention from the nonalcoholic parent.
   - Attention often revolved around the alcoholic parent. You did not receive the attention you required during times of crisis.
   - The nonalcoholic parent was often as inconsistent as the alcoholic parent was. Perhaps the nonalcoholic parent told you not to talk badly about the alcoholic. At other times, this parent may have called the alcoholic a no-good drunk.
   - The nonalcoholic parent may have expected you to assume more and more responsibility around the house as he or she took on more of the alcoholic's responsibilities.

B. *Background Material for Group Leader*
The following material provides the leader with additional information on the problems and concerns of a child in an alcoholic family.

Children who are raised in an alcoholic home are affected by their parents' alcoholism in many ways. These children do not receive consistent parenting or discipline. They do not learn to communicate openly about what is occurring at home or about how they feel about what is occurring. They grow up in an environment that is not conducive to the development of trust, good communication, or high self-esteem. Their homes are crisis oriented, and their dependency needs, as well as their need for stability, consistency, and structure, are not met.

Every child needs the predictability and consistency of people who will do what they say they will do, nurture them, and provide structure and discipline. The alcoholic parent demonstrates inconsistent behavior toward the child. He or she may seem angry when drinking, overly affectionate and permissive when sober, or vice versa. The emotional responses of the parent depend on the parent's mood and not on the child's behavior. The sudden shifts in the alcoholic's behavior bewilder the child. The parent may swing from violence to affection, which results in the child not knowing what to expect from the parent.

The alcoholic may break promises that he or she made to the child, thus causing the child to swing emotionally from high hopes to bitter disappointment. The parent may feel guilty later and try to make it up to the child by being overly lenient.

This behavior affects the child's ability to develop trust and eventually leads to problems concerning closeness and intimacy. The child grows up without the security or consistent love and warmth necessary for growth.

If it is the mother who drinks and if she is the primary caretaker, her behavior may interfere with her ability to provide physical care and emotional nurturing. The child may be subject to physical neglect. Such behavior also affects the child's ability to form close relationships later in life or to feel secure about him- or herself.

The alcoholic parent may be negligent because of his or her drinking. Children may be left unsupervised while the parent sleeps off a hangover. The parent may drive with the children in the automobile when he or she is intoxicated, or the children may have to wait alone for hours in the car outside a bar while the parent is inside drinking.

Children often must assume the role of parent at an early age because of their parents' alcoholism. The eldest child may be asked

14

to stay home from school to watch the younger children because Mom is hung over. The children become preoccupied with worrying about the next episode of excessive drinking or, for example, whether Dad will hit Mom. If both parents are alcoholics, the children must learn to take care of themselves and their parents. The children "grow up" too quickly and do not learn how to play or relax. They feel insecure because they are forced to assume adult roles without having yet acquired adult skills. Because they do not experience what it is like to be taken care of and only learn to take care of others, adult children of alcoholics tend to become involved in other dependent relationships in their adult years. They become overly responsible for the needs of others and out of touch with their own needs.

Time should be allowed for questions before continuing.

C. *Exercise Three*
   1. Objective: To increase awareness of how growing up in an alcoholic home is not conducive to the building of positive self-esteem in the child.
   2. Break into dyads.
   3. Ask members: How does growing up in an alcoholic home create low self-esteem?
   4. Discuss the following points as a group:
      - Children obtain self-esteem from their parents; parents help determine how the child will eventually feel about him- or herself.
      - Both the alcoholic and nonalcoholic parent are often overly critical and perfectionistic.
      - Nothing the child does is good enough. For example, he or she is told that A's on the report card should be A pluses.
      - Criticism is rarely constructive and is usually in the form of a personal attack.
      - Parents overreact to small things such as spilling the milk and respond by humiliating or demeaning the child, perhaps calling the child stupid or clumsy.
      - The child may be humiliated in front of friends or family members.
      - The child may be verbally or physically abused. The child begins to believe that he or she is bad and deserves this treatment or learns to hate the parent(s) for the abuse and feels that he or she is a bad person for hating the parent(s).
      - The child blames him- or herself for the parent's drinking or abusiveness, which in turn is reinforced by the alcoholic, who

15

also blames the child for the drinking behavior.

- The child develops low self-esteem from not receiving enough positive attention from his or her parents. The child feels unvalued and that his or her needs are less important than the alcoholic's needs.
- The child feels inadequate when performing adult tasks without adult skills.
- Most important, the child develops low self-esteem because he or she feels loved for what he or she does and not for who he or she is. Since perfection is the standard communicated at home, the child can never do enough or be good enough. The child judges him- or herself according to these high standards and always falls short. Successes build confidence but not self-esteem. Because self-esteem comes from being loved for who one is and because who the child is is never good enough, the child either pushes him- or herself to do more or gives up completely. The child never receives validation of his or her feelings, needs, or self—a key factor in the development of low self-esteem.

D. *Debrief*

Ask members if they have any questions. Ask them how they felt while discussing some of these topics. Thank them for sharing and tell them that it is often difficult and painful for adult children of alcoholics to discuss their childhood and to get in touch with their feelings. However, doing so is the beginning of recovery and the eventual acceptance of themselves.

REFERENCES

1. Charles Deutsch, *Broken Bottles, Broken Dreams* (New York: Teachers College Press, 1982), p. 7.
2. Sharon Wegscheider, "Children of Alcoholics Caught in Family Trap," *Focus on Alcohol and Drug Issues* 2 (May–June 1979): 8
3. James R. McKay, "Clinical Obervations on Adolescent Problem Drinkers," *Quarterly Studies on Alcohol* 22 (1961): 128–30; James R. McKay, "Juvenile Delinquency and Drinking Behavior," *Journal of Health and Social Behavior* 4 (Winter 1963): 282.
4. Claudia Black, *It Will Never Happen to Me!* (Denver: ACT, 1981).

HANDOUT—SESSION 1

Suggested Reading List

Beattie, Melody. *Codependent No More*. Center City, Minn.: Hazelden, 1987.

Black, Claudia. *It Will Never Happen to Me!* Denver: ACT, 1981.

Black, Claudia. *Repeat After Me*. Denver: ACT, 1985.

Deutsch, Charles. *Broken Bottles, Broken Dreams*. New York: Teachers College Press, 1982.

Forewood, Susan, and Joan Torres. *Men Who Hate Women and the Women Who Love Them*. New York: Bantam, 1986.

Hay, Louise. *You Can Heal Your Life*. Santa Monica, Calif.: Hay House, Inc., 1904.

Lerner, Rokelle. *Daily Affirmations for Adult Children of Alcoholics*. Pompano Beach, Fla.: Health Communications, 1985.

Milton, James, and Katherine Ketcham. *Under the Influence*. New York: Bantam, 1981.

Norwood, Robin. *Letters from Women Who Love Too Much*. New York: Pocket Books, 1988.

Norwood, Robin, and Jeremy P. Torcher. *Women Who Love Too Much*. New York: St. Martin's Press, 1985.

O, Pat. *Afraid to Live, Afraid to Die*. Center City, Minn.: Hazelden, 1983.

Peck, M. Scott, M.D. *The Road Less Traveled*. New York: Simon and Schuster, 1978.

This New Day by an Anonymous ACOA. Rockaway, N.J.: Quotidian, 1985.

Scales, Cynthia. *Potato Chips for Breakfast*. Rockaway, N.J.: Quotidian, 1986.

Wegscheider, Sharon. *Another Chance*. Palo Alto, Calif.: Science and Behavior Books, 1981.

Whitfield, Charles L. *Healing the Child Within*. Pompano Beach, Fla.: Health Communications, 1987.

Woititz, Janet Geringer. *Adult Children of Alcoholics*. Hollywood, Fla.: Health Communications, 1983.

Woititz, Janet Geringer. *Struggle for Intimacy*. Pompano Beach, Fla.: Health Communications, 1985.

Viorst, Judith. *Necessary Losses*. New York: Ballantine, 1986.

Note: The following is a primary source for literature on adult children of alcoholics:

Perrin & Treggett Booksellers
P.O. Box 190
Rutherford, N.J. 07070
800-321-7912 or 201-777-2277

HANDOUT—SESSION 1

Adult Children of Alcoholics

Objectives: This group was designed for individuals, now of adult age, who grew up in an alcoholic home. The purpose of this group is to increase the awareness of these individuals on the special issues they have as adult children of alcoholics. Although the intent of the group is not to diagnose or treat, resources will be provided for treatment and support.

Session 1: Background Information on Adult Children of Alcoholics and the Alcoholic Home
- Introduction
- Identification of common interests and concerns
- Statistics and general information on adult children of alcoholics
- How the child is affected by the alcoholic parent's behavior
- Parental inconsistency
- How growing up in an alcoholic family creates low self-esteem

Session 2: The Rules of the Home: Don't Talk, Don't Feel, Don't Trust
- How a child learns not to talk
- Why the alcoholic and nonalcoholic spouse cannot talk honestly
- Denial as the family's greatest defense
- Double messages about honesty
- How a child learns not to feel
- How denial of feelings results in becoming out of touch with oneself
- How a child learns not to trust

Session 3: Understanding Your Feelings
- One's feelings as a child in the alcoholic home
- "Stuffing one's feelings" as an adult
- Understanding your feelings as an adult

- Why is it good to express feelings?
- What are the positive results of expressing anger appropriately?
- Owning one's anger as a child and as an adult
- Identifying one's fears as a child
- Understanding feelings of guilt as a child and as an adult

Session 4:   The Roles within the Home That Get Carried Into Adulthood
- The responsible child or family hero
- How being overly responsible negatively affects the child and later the adult
- Adult children have difficulty having fun and take themselves very seriously
- The family scapegoat or the acting-out child
- The lost child or the adjuster

Session 5:   The Mascot and the Placater
- The mascot
- The placater
- Reshaping one's role
- How each role may set the individual up for a dependency on alcohol
- How one's role in the home influences the choice of a mate
- Why adult children tend to seek out other compulsive personalities for intimate relationships

Session 6:   Adult-Child Issues
- Adult children of alcoholics feel isolated and afraid of people
- Adult children of alcoholics feel different from other people
- Adult children of alcoholics overreact to changes over which they have no control
- Fear of angry people and any personal criticism
- Tendency to avoid conflict, or aggravate it, but rarely deal with it
- Addiction to excitement

Session 7:   Adult-Child Issues
- Fear of abandonment as a child

- Fear of abandonment as an adult
- Adult children of alcoholics are loyal even in the face of evidence that the loyalty is undeserved
- Adult children have difficulty with intimate relationships

Session 8: Resources for Recovery, Treatment, and Self-Help Groups For Adult Children of Alcoholics
- Impulsive behavior
- Treatment for adult children of alcoholics
- Treatment for the substance-addicted adult child
- ACOA
- Al-Anon

SESSION 2

OBJECTIVES: To increase members' awareness of the rules of the alcoholic home: "Don't Talk, Don't Feel, Don't Trust."[1]
To help members understand their difficulties in feeling, communicating, and trusting others.
To increase group members' awareness of their tendency to isolate themselves from other people.

I. OPENING THE SESSION

A. Review of Session 1: Ask members if they wish to comment on previous week's session.

B. Brief overview of Session 2.

II. "DON'T TALK"

A. *Mini-Lecture: How Does a Child Learn Not to Talk?*
The first thing you learned as children in an alcoholic home is not to talk honestly. You learned at a young age not to talk about your parent's alcoholism, because it was met with denial. Your parents tried to minimize or rationalize the problem; for example, you were told, "Dad drinks because he's been working too hard lately."[2]

As children in an alcoholic home, you learned not to talk because no one else in the family talked honestly about the problem in the home. You learned not to discuss "real" issues. If you questioned the non-drinking parent about the alcoholic's behavior, he or she denied or tried to rationalize the problem. "It is easier to invent reasons other than alcoholism to explain crazy behavior."[3]

If you broached the subject of alcoholism, your opinions were either behaviorally or verbally discounted. Perhaps you were told, "Don't say that about your Dad." Parents discount the child by not responding to or validating what is said, or by forbidding discussion.*

As children in an alcoholic home, you did not talk honestly because you were afraid of the consequences. You were afraid that you would receive an angry response, be hit or punished, or not be believed.*

You did not talk about your concerns because you received mixed messages from your parents. They may have told you that you could come to them with your problems; then when you did, they may have said, "You're always bothering me" or "Just don't worry about it." Such inconsistency confused you.

You may not have talked about what went on at home because you felt ashamed.

You may have felt disloyal and as though you were betraying the family by telling someone outside the home. You may have thought that saying that Mom or Dad did something bad was the same as saying that they were bad. Like your parents, you saw everything in terms of black and white. You did not understand that you could love your parents but hate their behavior, that one feeling did not eradicate another. You did not learn that having contradictory feelings did not make you "crazy." You did not learn that expressing hurt or anger toward a parent was not the same as betraying them.*

Ask group members if they have any questions.

B. *Exercise One*
   1. Objective: To increase members' awareness of how their parents handled their attempts to talk about the problem in the home.
   2. Break into dyads.
   3. Ask members to do the following: Try to remember a time when you attempted to talk to someone in your family about how you felt about the alcoholic's behavior or about a problem in the home that you felt concerned about. How was it handled? Think of an excuse or a rationalization that your parents gave you as a child to explain the behavior of the alcoholic parent.
   4. Discuss these topics as a group.

C. *Mini-Lecture: Why Your Parents Could Not Talk Honestly about the Alcoholic's Behavior: The Problems Created by His or Her Drinking*

For both the alcoholic and nonalcoholic parent, not talking about the alcoholic's behavior is part of the denial process.* Denial is the major defense used by the alcoholic and the spouse in an alcoholic family

24

system. Part of the denial process is believing that if the problem is not brought into the open, it will go away.[4] Thus denial allows the person not to think about or confront the problem.

Claudia Black related an incident experienced by a nine-year-old client in which he was left alone with his alcoholic father. The father passed out, hit his head on the coffee table, and began bleeding. When the boy's mother and older sister returned, they immediately ran to take care of the father. No one asked the boy how long Dad had been like this or what had happened. Nothing was said to the boy, and the boy said nothing to his mother. When Black asked the mother why she had not said anything, the mother said, "My son hadn't said anything to me. I hoped he hadn't noticed."[5]

"If I am a child growing up in an alcoholic home, my parents can't be honest with me because they can't be honest with themselves." The nonalcoholic parent loses his or her ability to be honest with the child. He or she cannot be honest because one bit of honesty would lead to the next. One would have to look back at the many years of disappointment and compromise. This would overwhelm the nonalcoholic spouse with feelings of helplessness and powerlessness. He or she cannot talk honestly, because doing so would require dealing with the reality of the situation all alone, thus creating an even deeper sense of futility and hopelessness. Denial creates a false sense of hope.*

The alcoholic is also unable to talk honestly. The alcoholic has a psychological dependency as well as a physiological addiction.* Alcoholics cannot consistently control their drinking or predict their behavior once they start to drink. Eventually, drinking becomes a compulsion rather than a choice.

"If I'm an alcoholic, I'm dependent on the drug alcohol. I have a need to drink. This makes me feel guilty and remorseful. If I drink, I don't feel all those things. If I'm honest, I'll have to take a look at the reality of my life, and at the consequences of my drinking behavior. But I need to drink, so that's not a safe thing to do. And I would have to do that all alone." It is too depressing for the alcoholic to look at life realistically. Honesty diminishes for both the alcoholic and the spouse as the alcoholism progresses. "The alcoholic and the family continue to minimize, rationalize and deny."*

Ask group members if they have questions.

25

D. *Mini-Lecture: Always Tell the Truth; I Don't Want to Know*
   Although as a child you were told to always tell the truth, you
   learned that eveyone else lied about the alcoholic's drinking. The
   family denied the problem, insisted that everything was all right and
   that the drinking behavior of the alcoholic was normal and under
   control. The coalcoholic parent covered and made excuses for the
   alcoholic. The alcoholic also broke promises. Thus, as adult children
   of alcoholics, lying is an issue in your lives because it was a norm in
   your homes when you were children. Lying may be a tool that you
   learned to use in order to cope. Perhaps you have learned to lie to
   yourself and others about how you feel and how things were or are.

   As children in an alcoholic home you were also given a contradictory
   message. You were told to always tell the truth; yet when you did,
   your parents acted as if they didn't want to know. You were punished
   if you did not tell the truth and were found out but were often made
   to feel as though you were burdening your parents when you told
   them about a problem situation. Also, your parents may have
   ignored your problems because they were too preoccupied with their
   own.[6]

   Ask members if they have questions.

III. "DON'T FEEL"

A. *Mini-Lecture: Why Do Adult Children of Alcoholics Find It Difficult
   to Talk about or Be in Touch with Their Feelings?*
   As adults you find it difficult to talk about your feelings because you
   are scared to death of your feelings. You have learned to cope by
   "stuffing" (that is, repressing) your painful feelings of hurt, anger,
   and sadness. When you sometimes do get in touch with feelings of
   past anger or sadness, the pain may be overwhelming because it has
   been repressed for so long. You may be afraid that if you allow yourselves to feel sad, you will never stop crying, or that if you allow yourselves to be angry, you will lose control.*

   As adult children, you are afraid of your feelings because you equate
   expression of emotion with loss of control. In the alcoholic home, feelings are either not expressed or expressed in a volatile way. As a
   child you never heard feelings talked about. You never saw the
   adults in the home actually sit down and discuss a problem or work it
   through. Anger was either repressed or expressed in an explosive
   manner. Violence or screaming may have caused you to equate the

expression of anger with loss of control. You were not exposed to any positive models for handling anger or conflict.*

B. *Mini-Lecture: "Don't Feel"*

As children you learned not to feel in the same way you learned not to talk—through lack of validation and lack of role models. No one else in your family talked about feelings; feelings were either repressed or expressed explosively.

By the time a child who is raised in an alcoholic home reaches the age of nine, he or she already has a well-developed system of denial. The child learns to deny both feelings and perceptions about what is going on at home. They learn to "stuff" or repress their feelings, because doing so is less painful than having to deal with them all by themselves. Having had to deny the reality of the home situation when they were young, adult children of alcoholics become very out of touch with their feelings.*

As adult children of alcoholics, you were made to feel guilty about how you felt. You felt guilty about being angry at Dad for his drinking and angry at Mom for staying with Dad, or vice versa. You may have felt guilty about your feelings in general. Your nonalcoholic parent did not know how to validate your feelings by saying, "I know just how you feel; I get upset with your Mom (or Dad) when she (or he) is drinking, too." Instead, you heard "Don't talk about your father that way" or "Don't get so upset; everything will be all right."*

Because you did not receive validation of your feelings and perceived others as not understanding or as unwilling to listen, you became more isolated as a child. You learned not to talk about your feelings, to keep your feelings inside, and eventually not to feel your feelings. Eventually, instead of keeping more feelings in, you learned to cut them off. You became disconnected and out of touch with yourself and your feelings.*

As adult children of alcoholics, you cannot express your feelings because they are so deeply repressed. You may have even lost the ability to identify your feelings. As children, you learned to lump your feelings together; that is, you were always angry, always sad, always anxious or afraid. You may have lost access to your full range of feelings. As adults, you may not be able to differentiate hurt from sadness or anger. Although being out of touch with your feelings gave you a sense of psychological safety as a child, it interferes with your ability to communicate and be honest with yourself and with others as adults.*

C. *Exercise Two*
   1. Objective: To increase members' awareness of what it felt like to grow up in an alcoholic home.
   2. Full group exercise.
   3. Ask the group to think of words or adjectives that describe either how they felt or what it felt like in general growing up in an alcoholic home.
   4. List the following words on a flip chart:

scared	depressed
frightened	sad
confused	unfair
frustrated	miserable
disappointed	bizarre
painful	demeaned
angry	degraded
out of control	hopeless
hateful	unsafe
inconsistent	fearful
unpredictable	unloved
extemely lonely	neglected
isolated	guilty

IV. "DON'T TRUST"

A. *Mini-Lecture: "Don't Trust"*
   For a child to develop trust and feel secure, certain factors must be present:
   1. Predictability
   2. Consistency
   3. Ability to depend on those around you to do what they say they will do

As a child you could not trust adults who were close to you to take care of you physically or emotionally in a consistent fashion. Your parents could be loving one minute and rejecting the next, overly strict or overly lenient. A vast discrepancy existed between sober and drunk behavior, which resulted in your not knowing what to expect from your parents. This behavior confused you as a child.

It is difficult to develop trust when one cannot rely on people to be open and honest. Both the alcoholic and spouse lose their ability to be honest as the illness progresses. The alcoholic needs to rationalize his or her drinking in order to continue the drinking. The spouse needs to rationalize that everything is under control in order to deal with the increased sense of loss of control. Because neither parent is honest, the child never receives validation of his or her feelings, which results in the child never learning to trust his or her own perception or judgment. Because of this lack of validation, adult children of alcoholics end up distrusting their own thoughts and feelings and not following their own instincts.[7]

Part of being able to trust is being able to feel safe emotionally and physically with those closest to you. As children, you did not experience what it was like to reach out and have your trust rewarded. It is difficult to trust a person who repeatedly embarrasses, humiliates, disappoints, or physically or emotionally abuses you.[8] It is not enough for parents to tell their children that they love them; they must demonstrate that love.

B. *Exercise Three*
 1. Objective: To increase members' awareness of their difficulties with trust.
 2. Full group discussion.
 3. Ask members what made them distrust their parents when they were children. "As a child, what kinds of things couldn't you trust your parents to do?"
 4. Ask members if they find it difficult to trust others now.
 5. Discuss the following points as a group. As a child you could not trust Mom or Dad
    - not to drink
    - to keep promises
    - to be home at night
    - not to fight
    - not to be fired due to drinking
    - to take time to listen to your problems or play with you
    - to be understanding
 6. Allow questions before closing.

REFERENCES

1. Claudia Black, *It Will Never Happen To Me!* (Denver: ACT, 1981), pp. 31–49.
2. Ibid., p. 33.
3. Ibid., p. 34.
4. Black, *It Will Never Happen To Me!*, p. 35.
5. Ibid.
6. Janet Geringer Woititz, *Adult Children of Alcoholics* (Pompano Beach, Fla.: Health Communications, 1983), pp. 20, 32–33.
7. Black, *It Will Never Happen To Me!*, p. 42.
8. Ibid., p. 41.

SESSION 3

OBJECTIVES: To help members understand their feelings by increasing their awareness of the feelings of sadness, fear, anger, guilt, and embarrassment that they experienced as children in an alcoholic home. To understand how their childhood experience affects their experience and expression of feelings as adults.

I. OPENING THE SESSION

A. Review of Session 2: Ask members if they wish to comment on previous week's session.

B. Brief overview of Session 3.

II. UNDERSTANDING YOUR FEELINGS AS A CHILD AND AN ADULT

A. *Exercise One*
1. Objectives: To increase members' awareness of their fears and what they felt sad, angry, embarrassed, guilty, or confused about as a child. The purpose of this exercise is to validate members' feelings by focusing first on feelings they experienced in the past and then on how they experience these feelings now.
2. Do exercise as a full group.
3. As a child, what kinds of things occurred in your home that made you feel:
   a. afraid
   b. sad
   c. angry
   d. embarrassed
   e. guilty
   f. confused
4. List answers on a flip chart and include the following points in the discussion:[1]
   a. Afraid
      • when your parents fought

- that you might be hit or yelled at
- that your mother or father would get killed while driving drunk
- that your parents would never get better
- that your mother or father would not come home at night
- that your mother or father would embarrass you
- to say no for fear that your mother or father would drink or that you would be punished
- that your parents did not love you

b. Sad
- because your family was often unhappy
- because your mother was often crying
- because your father could not keep a job
- when you had to sit in the car for hours because your mother or father was in a bar
- when your parents did not have time to listen to you or play with you

c. Angry
- at your mother or father for making promises and always breaking them
- at your mother or father for drinking
- at your mother for making excuses for your father's drinking
- at others for calling your parent a drunk
- at your mother or father for showing up drunk at your school play or not showing up at all

d. Embarrassed
- because your parents did not attend school functions
- or because when they did attend, they were intoxicated
- because your mother or father looked sloppy and ungroomed
- because your father or mother was drinking when you came home with a friend
- because your mother or father was loud at parties

e. Guilty
- for sometimes feeling angry at and hating people you were supposed to love
- for feeling ashamed of your parents
- for never being able to please your mother or father
- for perhaps thinking that if you were better at sports or school work, your parents would not drink

f. Confused
- about why your mother or father drank so much

32

- because your mother or father was inconsistent, perhaps giving you permission to go out early in the day, then later forgetting what he or she had said because he or she was drinking
- because your mother or father seemed to love you at times but was abusive at other times

5. Ask group if they have questions.

B. *Mini-Lecture: "Stuffing" One's Feelings*

"Stuffing" one's feelings is a common expression used with adult children of alcoholics. It refers to learning as a child and later as an adult not to express or feel one's feelings because they are too painful. A major issue for adult children of alcoholics is that they have learned to "stuff" their feelings from their traumatic childhoods and have lost the ability to feel or express these feelings because of the pain that results. This repression of feelings includes good feelings such as joy and happiness. Being out of touch with one's feelings is a basic form of denial. However, one can only stuff feelings for so long. Anger turned inward results in depression, and anger that accumulates may result in violence or rage. Although as adult children you may not always be in touch with or feel your feelings, you still react to them. Repression of your feelings can cause you to overreact to situations without your being aware of why you feel so intensely or so threatened over a seemingly innocuous event. Overreaction then serves to reinforce your tendency to equate emotional expression with loss of control.

As stated above, stuffing one's feelings is a basic form of denial. At an early age and now as an adult, you learned to tell others that you were not really disappointed, that you really did not feel hurt or angry. You learned to reassure others that you were not really upset. You became so understanding of why others could not be there for you, that you were able to "understand away" your own feelings.[2] If you could find an excuse for the other person's behavior, then you wouldn't have to feel the hurt or anger caused by that behavior. To deny that someone has upset you is to deny that someone has the power to interfere with your sense of control or to make you feel vulnerable.

As adult children you do not know how to express positive feelings. Perhaps you never heard your parents say "I love you" or "Nice job."

Stuffing your feelings makes it difficult for you to establish honest

33

and open relationships as an adult. Communication is a crucial element in any relationship. In order to communicate how you feel, you must first be in touch with your feelings.

An important step toward recovery is to get back in touch with your feelings. You must learn to feel, accept, and express your feelings. Accepting both positive and negative feelings builds self-esteem.

Ask members if they have questions.

C. *Exercise Two*
   1. Objectives: To increase members' awareness of the benefits of expressing anger appropriately.
   2. Ask members to name some good things that can come out of expressing anger appropriately.
   3. Do exercise as a full group.
   4. Include the following points in the discussion:*
      - If you release your anger, you will not be immobilized or depressed by it.
      - Expressing anger diminishes its strength and its power to overwhelm.
      - If anger or conflict is discussed and dealt with, positive results may occur.
      - Expressing your anger makes you feel freer and less uptight.
      - If you are full of anger, you may not have room for other feelings. Expressing anger leaves room for softer feelings, such as sadness, joy, or happiness.
      - Feeling free to express negative as well as positive feelings in a relationship helps establish trust and intimacy with others.
      - Anger is a dominant emotion of children and adult children of alcoholics. It is natural for children who have been repeatedly disappointed, neglected, or abused by the people they love and need the most to feel angry. Their anger toward others can result in low self-esteem if they do not understand its roots, as anger is usually seen as a negative emotion and angry people as being "bad."
      - Because your feelings of anger, even if unexpressed, provoked a great deal of guilt and anxiety, you may have learned to deny these angry feelings.
      - As adult children you may be genuinely unaware of your rage toward your parents.
      - Some of you turned your anger inward and became depressed. You may feel a generalized and helpless sense of

rage, injustice, or deprivation. You may feel that life is not worth living.

- Some of you may not allow yourselves to feel any anger.
- You may not invest in anything emotionally so that nothing will matter enough to elicit an angry reaction.
- Some of you may have acted out your anger as children by releasing the rage you felt toward your parents on teachers, other children, or in acts of domestic violence as adults.
- Learning to express your anger in healthy and appropriate ways helps break the cycle of depression and volatility.

5. Discuss the following: It is important that you learn how to express your feelings appropriately. Your fear of expressing your feelings is usually worse than the reality of doing so.* Grief is another feeling that adult children of alcoholics are afraid to express, because they are afraid they will lose control. They fear that crying will lead to hysteria and anger to explosiveness.* However, crying can be a positive breakthrough for the adult child of an alcoholic, because it allows him or her to express grief and sadness for past hurts and losses.

Some of you are unable to cry because you received messages such as "If you don't stop crying, I'll really give you something to cry about" or "Crying doesn't change anything." Some adult children cry silently or when they are alone; others cry too easily or at inappropriate times, without understanding why they are crying or why they are overly sensitive.

As adult children of alcoholics, you must (1) understand that sometimes you need to cry, (2) give yourself permission to cry, (3) realize when you do feel sad, and (4) let another person be supportive.[3] Crying is a healthy release that can make you feel better. It is all right to cry and to share your grief with others. As adult children of alcoholics you must learn the positive value of expressing sadness and anger and learn how to do so appropriately.

D. *Exercise Three*
1. Objective: To help adult children of alcoholics identify and express their anger.
2. Do exercise as a full group (use handout)[4]
   - Make a list of things you could have been angry about as a child, for example, "I could have been angry at Dad for not

35

keeping his promises." Share this list with the group and discuss.

- Make a list of things that you could be, but are not, angry about as an adult, for example, "I could be angry at my parents for never getting sober. I could be angry when people take advantage of me." Discuss with the entire group.
- Cross out the words "I could be" and write "I am," "I was," or "I am still." Reflect to yourself how you feel right now. Acknowledging anger, as well as your other feelings, is a necessary part of recovery.

E. *Exercise Four*
1. Objective: To help group members get in touch with their fears as children and as adults.
2. Break into dyads.
3. Ask group members the following question: What did you fear as a child, and how did you handle your fear? What kinds of fears do you have now?
4. Discuss as a group. Include the following points in the discussion: As children you were afraid of being alone, getting hit, disapproval, abandonment, rejection.[5]
5. How did you cope with your fear as a child?
   - went to your room and cried
   - became angry
   - hid in a closet
   - asked a brother or sister for help
   - let others know you were afraid
6. How did you let others know about your fears? Did you wet your bed?
7. Discuss the following: As a child growing up in an alcoholic home, no one was available to you to validate your fears, help you express them, or put them in perspective. When you were falsely reassured that everything was all right, you only felt more alone. When a child is allowed to talk about his or her fears, the child feels less overwhelmed and less isolated.[6]

Although fear is an emotion that everyone experiences at one time or another in the course of growing up, you felt fearful most of the time. You grew up fearing the unknown and what would happen next, because you did not know when the alcoholic would drink or how he or she would act.[7]

"As adults, children of alcoholics often experience an overwhelming sense of fear."[8] Consequently, you are often unaware of what you are afraid of. Having grown up not knowing what to expect next, you continue to experience uncertainty and fear of the unknown as an adult. This fear of the unknown may prevent you from making positive changes or trying new things. This state of fear can be episodic or continual and may cause depression, isolation, and low self-esteem in the adult child.[9]

8. Ask group members if they have questions.

F. *Exercise Five*

1. Objectives: To increase members' awareness of what they felt guilty about as a child and how they may still live with this guilt as an adult.

2. Ask the group the following questions (use handout):[10]
   - What did you feel guilty about or blame yourself for as a child?
   - Upon reflection, is it realistic to expect a child to have behaved differently from the way you did or to have been able to handle the situation any better?
   - Do you still blame yourself for everything that goes wrong as an adult?

3. Include the following points in the discussion:[11]
   - You often felt guilty about your conflicting feelings toward your parents.
   - You probably thought that you should feel differently from the way you did.
   - You were told that you should always love and respect your parents, but your parents, especially the alcoholic parent, did not always behave in a way that evoked either love or respect.
   - Love consists of mutual sharing, trust, and respect. The inconsistent, disappointing, and abusive behavior of the alcoholic was not conducive to creating this kind of environment. Although you may have needed your parents, you did not necessarily love or trust them.
   - No one helped you not to feel guilty about your conflicting emotions. Your negative feelings were not validated. No one said, "I understand how you can feel that way about your father" or "You know you can love your dad, but still hate his drinking behavior" or "I hate it when your father acts that way too, although I love him when he does not drink."
   - You never learned that one feeling does not eradicate another. You can both love and be angry at your parents.

37

- Feelings are transitory. You may have felt guilty and confused because you hated your mother or father when they were abusive.
- You never learned that it was all right to feel and express both positive and negative feelings.
- If you had been allowed to express your feelings, you would have felt less guilty.
- Most of you loved your parents. A child's love can withstand a great deal of inconsistent and traumatic behavior from the parent. Your experiences with your parents were not all negative. Alcoholic parents are not drunk all the time.
- Your parent's alcoholism may not have been consistently disruptive to the family. You may have learned to love this parent during the early stages of his or her alcoholism, then felt confused as the illness progressed and the alcoholic became more rigid, angry, inconsistent, depressed, or absent.
- You did not know that even if you behaved in a way that upset your parents, they had other choices besides drinking or being abusive to handle the situation.
- You did not know that alcoholics are responsible for their own actions—a concept that is helpful for the entire family to understand.
- You were made to feel guilty about almost everything that went on in your home, including your parents' drinking. Children often assume that they have the power to affect what occurs around them. However, they have very little power in an alcoholic environment.
- Just as children in a nonalcoholic family blame themselves and need reassurance when their parents get divorced, children in an alcoholic home need to be reassured by their parents that they are not responsible for the alcoholic's drinking.
- You were not told that alcoholism is an illness. You did not know that you were not the cause of your parent's alcoholism and that you could not prevent it.
- You probably felt frustrated or helpless because your efforts failed to affect the alcoholic's drinking. No matter how well you behaved or how well you did at school or at sports, you could not cause, prevent, or stop your parent's drinking.
- You felt guilty because of your lack of power.
- You continue to carry the guilt feelings you experienced as children. As adults, you must separate that which you held yourself responsible for when you were a child from that which you hold yourself responsible for as an adult. You

must realize that children do not have the emotional, physical, and psychological abilities of an adult before you can rid yourself of the guilt and self-blame that you experienced as a child.

4. Ask members if they have questions.

REFERENCES

1. Claudia Black, *It Will Never Happen to Me!* (Denver: ACT, 1981), pp. 48–49.
2. Janet Woititz, "Intimate Relationships and Adult Children of Alcoholics," audiotape from the set *Families and Alcoholism* (Indianapolis: ACCESS, 1983).
3. Black, *It Will Never Happen to Me!*, pp. 111–12.
4. Ibid., pp. 117–18.
5. Ibid., p. 115.
6. Ibid., pp. 80–81.
7. Ibid., p. 80.
8. Ibid., p. 113.
9. Ibid., pp. 113–14.
10. Ibid., p. 121.
11. Ibid., pp. 82–85, 120–21.

HANDOUT—SESSION 3

Make a list of all the things that you could have been angry about as a child.

Example: I could have been angry at my dad for hitting my mom when she was drunk. I could have been angry the time my mom passed out on Christmas Eve.

1. _____
2. _____
3. _____
4. _____
5. _____

Make a list of things you could be but are not angry about as an adult.

Example: I could be angry at my dad for never getting sober. I could be angry when people take advantage of me.

1. _____
2. _____
3. _____
4. _____
5. _____

Cross out the words "I could be" and write "I am," "I was," or "I am still."

Example: I am still angry at my dad for hitting my mom when she was drunk. I am angry at my dad for never getting sober. I was angry the time my mom passed out on Christmas Eve. I am still angry at my mom for not listening to me when I told her Dad was drunk.

From Claudia Black, *It Will Never Happen to Me!* (Denver: ACT, 1981), pp. 117–18. Used with permission.

HANDOUT—SESSION 3

Think about the guilt that you still carry from childhood. Do you ever say "If only I had _____?" For example: "If only I had been more understanding," "gotten better grades at school so Dad wouldn't drink," or "protected Mom from Dad when he drank." What "if onlys" do you still ask yourself? As a child, if only I had:

1. _____
2. _____
3. _____
4. _____

Think about when you were a teenager. For example: "If only I had not run around with such a wild crowd," "spent more time at home instead of with my friends," or "done better at school." As a teenager, if only I had:

1. _____
2. _____
3. _____
4. _____

Think about your responses. Would any other six-year-old, twelve-year-old, or eighteen-year-old who was in the same situation have behaved any differently? It is important that you realize that as children you only had the emotional, physical, and psychological abilities of a child so that you can rid yourself of guilt and self-blame for your parent's alcoholism.

From Claudia Black, *It Will Never Happen to Me!* (Denver: ACT, 1981), pp. 121–22. Used with permission.

SESSION 4

OBJECTIVE: To increase members' understanding of the various roles in the alcoholic family: the overly responsible child or family hero, the acting-out child or family scapegoat, and the lost child or the adjuster.

I. OPENING THE SESSION

A. Review of Session 3: Ask members if they wish to comment on previous week's session.

B. Brief overview of Session 4.

II. MINI-LECTURE

A. *Roles in the Home*
(Claudia Black says, "The words which best describe living in an alcoholic family are inconsistency and unpredictability."[1]) As alcoholism progressed in your home, so did inconsistency, unpredictability, confusion, and chaos. Other family members attempted to reinstate some stability in the home. Their behavior was aimed at making life somewhat easier and less painful and seemed to make sense at the time. However, their actions resulted in family members becoming locked into certain coping roles or ways of behavior.[2] A functional family system has clearly defined, yet flexible, roles within the family. For example, Dad may help with the children, or Mom may work outside the home. When children are raised in a more flexible family system, they develop the ability to adopt various roles. They learn how to be responsible, how to organize, how to develop realistic goals, and how to play and enjoy themselves. "Children growing up in alcoholic homes seldom learn to assume the combinations of roles which mold healthy personalities. Instead they become locked into roles based on their perception of what they need to do to 'survive' and to bring some stability to their lives."[3]

The majority of children who grow up in alcoholic homes tend to appear normal. As children, most of you probably did not exhibit problematic behavior or adjustment problems. Although many of the children who are seen by school counselors, helping professionals, or the juvenile system are children from alcoholic homes, the vast majority of children from alcoholic homes do not draw attention to themselves and are therefore a neglected population. There are reasons for this "normal" behavior: if they appear to be like everyone else and if they do not draw attention to themselves through problematic behavior, they will look good, be ignored, and not draw attention to the problem in the home.[4]

Children who are raised in an alcoholic family usually adopt one or a combination of the following roles: the responsible child, the adjuster, the placater, or the family mascot.

B. *Overly Responsible Child or Family Hero*
These children assume responsibility not only for themselves, but for other members of the family as well. In order to provide the structure and consistency that is so sorely lacking in the family, they learn to become organized, goal oriented, and self-disciplined. These children are nine going on thirty years old.[5] They become household "top sergeants" and learn to manipulate people in positive ways.* They may take charge of the care of younger brothers and sisters or may assign chores and make sure they are carried out. These children have good leadership ability and learn to do things for themselves at an early age. They often focus on tangible, concrete tasks, such as taking out the garbage or doing the laundry, because these are the aspects of their lives that they can have some control over. They seldom misbehave and take on many of the household and parenting responsibilities. "Sometimes, responsible children are directed to assume this role; other times, they assume the role voluntarily."[6] Sometimes an older child might be expected to stay home from school to take care of the younger children if his or her mother has been drinking. Other times a child may assume the caretaker role without being asked.

Playing the overly responsible role gives the child a sense of control and increases the stability in the home. The child may also receive praise and recognition from parents and relatives. To outsiders, the overly responsible child appears extremely dependable, serious, or mature.[7] In *Adult Children of Alcoholics*, Janet Woititz provides the following example:

44

"Look at Emily, isn't she remarkable? She's the most responsible child I've ever seen. Wish I had one like that at home." If you were Emily, you smiled, felt good, and enjoyed getting the praise. You probably didn't allow yourself to think, "I wish my parents thought I was terrific. I wish I could be good enough for them." And you certainly didn't allow yourself to think, "well if I didn't do it, who would?" To an outsider looking in, you were simply a remarkable little child. And the truth of the matter is, you were. They just didn't see the whole picture.[8]

The overly responsible child, or family hero, has many admirers, but few close friends. He or she is often resented by peers and siblings for his or her achievements and competitiveness. "Heroes" need to feel in control and have great difficulty accepting criticism and supervision. This child is well rewarded by teachers and other adults for his or her behavior. Teachers tend to equate achievement with healthy adjustment and assume that children who do well academically have fewer critical emotional needs than do children who do poorly. If the child ever breaks out of this role and occasionally rebels, he or she is told "You should know better." Once the child sublimates his or her angry feelings, the praise starts rolling in again.[9]

III. EXERCISES

A. *Exercise One*
1. Objective: To increase members' awareness of how they handled responsibility as a child and how this has affected them.
2. Break into dyads and ask the following questions: As a child, what were your responsibilities in the home? Looking back, do you think that some of these responsibilities should have rightfully belonged to your parents? How was having too much responsibility as a child detrimental to your own growth?
   a. as a child?
   b. as an adult?
3. Discuss questions as a group.
4. Include the following points:
   a. *Effects on the child*
      - In taking on so many responsibilities at a young age, you did not get to experience what it was like to be a child or to be childlike.
      - You did not learn how to be relaxed, playful, or sponta-

45

neous because of the constant tension in your home.

- You did not learn how to have fun, or you may not have had time to have fun.
- You always felt inadequate because you were doing adult tasks without adult skills.
- You did not experience what it was like to be taken care of in a consistent way.
- Your own dependency needs did not get met.
- You did not learn to trust others to be there for you.
- Others did not treat your needs as if they were important or as though they took priority.
- You felt loved for what you did and not for who you were. Because you could not satisfy your parents' perfectionistic standards, you always felt that you were falling short, which resulted in low self-esteem.

b. *Effects on the adult* [10]

- You carried a lot of responsibility into adulthood.
- You experienced anxiety, tension, and felt separated from others.
- You may be extremely rigid in your independence and take pride in this trait.
- It is very difficult for you to allow yourself to depend on other people, because you have learned the only person upon whom you can depend is yourself.
- You may have become rigid and controlling as an adult. You may have a strong need to be in control and become anxious when you feel out of control in a relationship or situation. One of your greatest fears is loss of control.
- You may be very manipulative and competitive. You may not know how to lose and may only be comfortable in a "one-up" situation.
- You may not know how to listen to people or receive input.
- You feel alone in a crowd and different from other people. You may not know how to connect with others.
- As a result of having to take life so seriously when you were a child, you are very serious as an adult and do not know how to relax, be spontaneous, or have fun.
- You may feel empty inside when you are not attempting to achieve a goal or when you are not involved in some major project. As soon as you finish one project, you begin another because you feel unconnected and empty without a goal to focus on.

- The overly responsible child often becomes a compulsive workaholic as an adult. Because you received recognition when you were a child for what you did and not for who you were, you now feel that you can never do enough. You are a perfectionist. Achievement is your measure of self-worth.
- Although workaholics appear to be self-motivated, well adjusted, and successful, their need to be successful develops into a rigid behavior pattern that precludes satisfying other needs.[11]
- Workaholism is a defense against intimacy and against getting in touch with one's emotions. Working long hours crowds out the time needed for relationships, which can seriously affect your relationship with your partner or your children.[12]
- Workaholism is highly correlated with early fatal coronary disease.
- Workaholics may suffer from severe depression. They have a high rate of suicide during middle age; they feel empty inside despite their prestige and success.[13]
- Often, these people marry someone whom they can take care of or manage, including alcoholics. They need to feel in control and needed.

As children, overachievers hope that their achievements and personal selflessness will end their family's problems. When their achievements fail to solve their problems, they attribute this failure to their own inadequacies, rather than to the alcoholism, over which they had no control.[14] Their guilt serves as a defense against feelings of powerlessness.[15] Heroes are never satisfied with their own work, as children or adults, because it never brings about the desired results. They need to learn that they did not cause their parent's drinking and that they could never have brought their parent's drinking to an end, even through their own unwavering excellence. The family hero needs to learn to relax and stop trying to do it all. Either others will do it or it won't get done, but the world won't fall apart.[16]

B. *Exercise Two*
   1. Objective: To increase members' awareness of the manner in which they deal with responsibility.
   2. Break into dyads.
   3. Discuss the following questions: As an adult, do you see yourself

as being over- or underresponsible? Is it difficult for you either to
let others be responsible for themselves or to take responsibility
for your own self?
4. Discuss as a group.
5. Ask members if they have questions.

IV. MINI-LECTURE

A. *The Acting-Out Child or Family Scapegoat*
    The acting-out child, or family scapegoat, often becomes the object of
    the family's anger, disappointment, and frustrations. The rage and
    frustration that exist between the parents or among other family
    members are focused on this child. Often, this role is assumed by the
    second child.[17]

When a second child is born, the older sibling usually has already
played the role of hero. However, despite the first child's exemplary
behavior, the parent's drinking has become worse, perhaps both parents have become more ill, and conflict has escalated. Neither the
hero (first child) nor the parents feel that the first child's role has
been successful. Everyone in the family has continued to feel anger
and resentment. The older child has not made everything all right,
and the family members need a "safe" outlet for their anger. The second child, who, because of his or her age, can hardly outperform the
older child, conveniently fills this role. He or she may identify with
the alcoholic, who gets attention for shirking responsibility, upsetting
people, and needing others to care for him or her. In turn, this child's
behavior problems enable family members to believe that the family's
distress is caused by this child. The scapegoated child, rather than
the alcoholic, becomes the focus of the family's anger and need to
blame. The scapegoat receives a great deal of attention for his or her
negative behavior.

This child may be encouraged to act out because of inconsistent limits that are either laxer or stricter than those applied to the family
hero. The acting-out behavior is also reinforced by the attention the
child receives through verbal reproaches, physical punishment, and
the family's attempts to be understanding. Secretly, the family hopes
that if the scapegoat gets into enough trouble, the drinking will end
and the family will be united. The scapegoat provides the alcoholic
and other famiy members with someone to blame and with a diver-
sion from the alcoholic's drinking. The child's behavior reflects the
turmoil in the family. The scapegoat is often the most visible child in

the alcoholic home—the troublemaker. These children may do poorly at school, cut classes, talk back to teachers, break school rules, become teenage parents, drop out of school, or abuse drugs or alcohol.[18] They may exhibit socially unacceptable behavior and may end up in correctional facilities or mental hospitals.[19]

Scapegoats have extremely low self-esteem. They lack a strong parent–child relationship and gravitate toward peers who also have low self-esteem. They choose friends who share their defiance of authority[20] and find it difficult to communicate their feelings to adults in a healthy and constructive manner. They lack coping skills.[21]

These children are most likely to receive attention and help from professionals, such as teachers, social workers, police, judges, and chaplains. However, when they do get help it is often for their problematic behavior and not for their background in an alcoholic family.[22] These children see themselves, as the family sees them, as born losers.[23]

B. *Lost Child or the Adjuster*
The lost child, or the "adjuster" in the alcoholic family, is often a middle child. "While their brothers and sisters are locked into rigid and exaggerated roles, middle children are often given no role at all, no way in which to make their presence felt in the family," especially when the gap between them and younger children is small.[24] When the adjuster is born, the family is no longer looking for another hero or scapegoat, since the presence of these polarized roles has not made things better in the home and may have made things worse. The scapegoat in the family has demanded much attention and energy and helped to intensify conflict in the family. The alcoholic's drinking may be worse, and the nonalcoholic parent may be exhausted. When the "lost" child is born, he or she is not expected to transform the family, but rather to keep from disturbing its delicate balance.

The primary task of the lost child is to avoid conflict. The high level of tension and stress in the home is very threatening to him or her. Lost children conclude that if they cause additional stress, the family may crack at the seams. They are also unable to resolve conflicts among family members because of the already polarized situation.

The learned sense of powerlessness of the lost child comes from his or her experience of being involved in any form of conflict with the parent as a no-win situation. Lost children tend to withdraw emotionally and physically from the family. They draw as little attention to themselves as possible in order to avoid conflict. Withdrawal, in turn, results in feelings of loneliness, fear, and unimportance. These children feel that they are subject to the whims of other family members and that they are unable to express their strongest desires and fears.[25]

Unlike the responsible child, who takes charge of household tasks and makes decisions in order to feel in control, the adjuster learns to survive by simply adjusting to whatever happens in the home. When others in the home provide structure, younger children may not find it necessary to be responsible for themselves.[26]

These children believe that they have no control over their lives. Therefore, they do not understand the value of making decisions or working toward goals. They do not learn to make decisions, because no one respects the decisions that they make. Others make decisions for them, and consequently they do not develop confidence in their own ability to make decisions. Out of their sense of powerlessness, they learn not to initiate but to react to the events and circumstances of their lives. These children do not see options or alternatives. They find it difficult to follow through on decisions that they do make. They see themselves as victims. Adjusters learn not to invest emotionally in people, places, or things. Their attitude may be, "I don't need you; I don't need anyone." If their alcoholic parent disappoints them, they will tell others that it does not matter. They adjust to their disappointments and deny their importance.*

These children draw neither positive nor negative attention to themselves and are the least visible in the family. They often withdraw to their rooms or spend as much time out of the house as possible. They are often considered the most selfish child in the family because they have the least interaction with other family members. In school, these children are average. They do not demonstrate outstanding ability or failure. They do not assume leadership roles at school and are on the social periphery.[27]

Adjusters never learn that they have a right to question their parents' behavior or authority figures in general, even when their own safety is at stake.* They will sit in the car for hours waiting for their mother or father to come out of the bar. They may even learn to accept physical or sexual abuse.

50

V. Exercise Three

A. Objective: To increase members' awareness of how adjusters are negatively affected in adulthood by continuing to cope through adjusting.

B. Discuss the following question as a group: How might individuals who are adjusters be negatively affected by their coping role in adulthood? Include the following points:
- Adjusters often have no sense of identity or direction as adults because of their need to avoid disapproval and conflict by not making waves or rocking the boat.
- Adjusters lack purpose and a feeling of fulfillment in their lives.
- They find it difficult to say no even as adults and may not realize that they have that option.
- They find it difficult to see alternatives or to make decisions.*
- They find it difficult to take responsibility for their own behavior.
- They may prefer that others be in control, which allows them to continue feeling powerless or victimized.
- They may become addicted to crisis and excitement. As children, they constantly adjusted to the uproar caused by the alcoholic. As adults, they pick mates whose behavior also induces crisis, which perpetuates their childhood role of adapting to inconsistent people by adjusting.[28]

REFERENCES

1. Claudia Black, *It Will Never Happen to Me!* (Denver: ACT, 1981), p.13.
2. Ibid.
3. Ibid., p. 14.
4. Ibid., pp. 15–16.
5. Ibid., p. 16.
6. Black, *It Will Never Happen to Me!*, p. 18.
7. Ibid., pp. 19–20.
8. Janet Geringer Woititz, *Adult Children of Alcoholics* (Pompano Beach, Fla.: Health Communications, 1983), p. 8.
9. Charles Deutsch, *Broken Bottles, Broken Dreams* (New York: Teachers College Press, 1982), p. 60.
10. "Effects on the adult" are taken from the works of Claudia Black; Black, *It Will Never Happen to Me!;* and Deutsch, *Broken Bottles, Broken Dreams.*
11. Deutsch, *Broken Bottles, Broken Dreams*, p. 60.
12. Ibid.
13. Ibid.
14. Ibid.
15. Black, *It Will Never Happen to Me!*, p. 83.
16. Deutsch, *Broken Bottles, Broken Dreams*, p. 61.
17. Ibid., p. 62.
18. Ibid., p. 64.

19. Black, *It Will Never Happen to Me!*, p. 26.
20. Deutsch, *Broken Bottles, Broken Dreams*, p. 64
21. Black, *It Will Never Happen to Me!*, pp. 26–27.
22 Ibid., 67–68.
23. Deutsch, *Broken Bottles, Broken Dreams*, p. 64.
24. Ibid., pp. 66–67.
25. Ibid., pp. 67–68.
26. Black, *It Will Never Happen to Me!*, p. 21.
27. Ibid., pp. 21, 23.
28. Ibid., p. 58.

SESSION 5

OBJECTIVES: To increase members' awareness of the role of the mascot and the placater.
To help members understand how these roles are carried into adulthood, and how they affect the person's functioning and choice of a mate.
To increase members' awareness of how each role increases vulnerability to alcohol dependency.

I. OPENING THE SESSION

A. Review of Session 4: Ask members if they wish to comment on previous week's session.

B. Brief overview of Session 5.

II. MASCOT AND PLACATER ROLES

A. *Mini-Lecture: The Mascot Role*
The youngest child in the family often fills the mascot role. The family sees the mascot as an immature and fragile person in need of protection. As the baby of the family, the mascot may remain immature for a prolonged period. By caring for the mascot, older children may vicariously experience some of the care and protection that they missed when they were younger. The hero or overly responsible child welcomes having someone to take care of, the scapegoat welcomes having someone to like and to be liked by, and the lost child finds it easier to withdraw from the family when the mascot is around to divert the family's attention.[1]

The alcoholic and nonalcoholic parent may desire a second chance at childrearing. Their objective may be a happy rather than a successful child. In order to keep the child happy and protected, they may try to shield it from the "ugly side" of the family. The family may stop arguing when this child enters the room and may look to this child to make them laugh, to touch a soft spot, and to provide relief from anxiety. This child is encouraged to charm, cajole, or manipulate anyone who is being difficult, including the alcoholic. Mascots are responsible for diffusing explosive situations. They attempt to dispel tension wherever it occurs, even if they do not understand its source.[2]

In school, the mascot may become the class clown. The mascot's humor may be disruptive, or the kind that interrupts but is easily forgiven because of its charm (for example, flying paper airplanes). Mascots learn to manipulate and get what they want through charm, lying, wheedling, or cajoling.[3]

Ask members if they have questions.

B. *Exercise One*
   1. Objective: To understand the role of the mascot.
   2. Discuss the following questions as a group: Was there a mascot in your home, and if so, who played that role? What negative aspects of this role are carried into adulthood?
   3. Include the following points in the group discussion:
      As adults, mascots may be dependent on others. They often marry strong, silent persons and become "child" wives or "child" husbands. They cope by using their fragility and dependence to get others to take care of them. Mascots are at risk for alcohol or drug abuse, particularly minor tranquilizers, as a way to cope with anxiety or tension.[4]

C. *Mini-Lecture: The Placater Role*
The placater is the child who appears to be overly sensitive. This child's feelings get hurt easily; he or she laughs more, cries more, and shows a higher degree of emotional involvement with family members. Although the placating child is not necessarily the only sensitive child in the alcoholic home, he or she is perceived by the parents as the child who is most sensitive.[5]

The placater is the child who is most sensitive to everyone else's pain and will try to dilute the sadness, anger, and fears of other family members. This child might try to reassure the other children when the parents argue by singing to them or telling them a story to divert their attention. He or she may try to "make it up" to other siblings if Mom or Dad disappoints them. The placater helps family members minimize, rationalize, and deny. Claudia Black cites an instance in which a five-year-old boy tells his mother, "Don't worry, Mom, I won't remember all of this when I grow up."[6]

Placaters are usually liked by others and are considered nice persons. They spend most of their time trying to please and make others feel better. They are able to listen and demonstrate empathy and are well liked for these attributes. Friends often ask placaters for advice. They are viewed as knowing a lot and as not having problems of their own. Placaters are often called upon to settle disputes between others or to make decisions.*

Placaters tend not to disagree with others. They are first to apologize. An eleven-year-old child said to Black, "I just couldn't figure out why she was always drunk, and knew there must be something I did to make her so unhappy. So, I just tried to make it better by apologizing."[7]

Parents are often proud of the placater, seeing him or her as the unselfish child. This child makes it easy for the parents by not complaining and by hiding his or her disappointment.[8]

Ask members if they have questions.

D. *Exercise Two*
  1. Objective: To increase members' awareness of the role of the placater in the home.
  2. Break into dyads and discuss the following questions:
     - Who was the placater in your family?
     - If you were the placater, what was it like for you to have this role? If you were not the placater, how did you feel toward the person who assumed this role?
     - What are the negative effects of this role—first as a child and later as an adult?
  3. Discuss questions as a group; include the following information:
     As a child, the placater was overly sensitive to everyone else's needs, and continues to take care of others as an adult. Placaters tend to marry persons who are alcoholic, emotionally ill, or extremely dependent. Many may enter into the helping professions where they can attend to the pain of others.

"Adults who grow up in the roles of placaters typically go through years of adulthood never seriously considering what they want."[9] They discount their own needs. They have an overdeveloped sense of responsibility and find it easier to be concerned with others than with themselves. This enables them not to take responsibility for identifying and finding ways to meet their own needs. "They have perfected the inability to give to themselves."[10] As a result, they may never get what they want from life.

Growing up in an alcoholic home, the placater learns not to focus on his or her own needs or wants because they are not consistently validated or met. In order to survive emotionally these children learn to focus on and give their time, energy, and empathy to others. They become compulsive givers who feel guilty when they say no. Although giving to others is obviously not a bad thing in itself, doing so at the expense of one's own well-being is destructive.[11]

As adults, placaters are often depressed. They usually do not have equal relationships with others. They usually give too much and avoid putting themselves in positions in which they receive from others. In personal relationships, they often seek out people who are takers, people who do not want to share themselves emotionally, and people who cannot talk about their feelings.[12] As adults, placaters often feel isolated because they are unable to communicate their needs.

E. *Mini-Lecture: Reshaping One's Role*
It is important that adult placaters gain an understanding of the word "selfish." Since the placater's role has always been that of the sensitive listener who attends to the needs of others, it is natural that the placater feels guilty for focusing on him- or herself during the initial stages of recovery. One woman in her thirties said, "When I decide to put myself first for a change, I feel very guilty and have trouble differentiating between putting myself first and being selfish." Part of the recovery process is learning to give to oneself, which is not a bad thing.[13]

Adult placaters should attempt to give themselves newer, more positive, and healthier messages:[14]
- "My needs are important."
- "It is OK to put my own well-being first."
- "I don't have to take care of everyone else."
- "Others can lend support to those who need it when I am not willing to be available."
- "I have choices about how I respond to people."
- "I'm not guilty because others feel bad."
- "I deserve to be given a thank-you."
- "I enjoy receiving praise."

56

When placaters let go of having to be totally giving, they then have more energy left to receive. As you work on changing your behavior patterns, others will begin to respond to you differently. The overly responsible individual must learn to become more spontaneous and less controlling, the adjuster needs to become more assertive and to make decisions, and the placater must be more giving to him- or herself. Some people may welcome these changes in you, others may attempt to manipulate you so that they can continue to have their needs met. Remember that even though your changing may threaten others, these changes will result in an increased sense of wholeness.[15]

Ask members if they have questions.

F. *Exercise Three*
    1. Objective: To increase members' awareness of which new message from the Reshaping One's Role mini-lecture they most need to work on.
    2. Write messages on a flip chart.
    3. Break into dyads.
    4. Ask members to discuss new messages.
    5. Discuss as a full group.

III. IMPACT OF PARENTAL ALCOHOLISM ON ONE'S OWN DRINKING HABITS AND TENDENCIES TOWARD ADDICTIVE RELATIONSHIPS

A. *Mini-Lecture: A Family Illness*
Alcoholism is a family illness. Not only is it an illness that affects everyone in the family, it is an illness that runs in families. "Rarely do we see a case in isolation."[16] Usually a generational history of alcoholism can be found, although in some cases it may skip a generation. Fifty percent of all alcoholics have at least one alcoholic parent.[17]

Children of alcoholics run a higher risk of developing alcoholism than do children from nonalcoholic families, probably because of a combination of genetic and environmental factors.[18] Adult children of alcoholics are predisposed to developing alcoholism in a number of ways. They suffer from low self-esteem, a sense of isolation, and an inability to connect with other people because of the unspoken rules "don't talk, don't feel, don't trust." Alcohol can temporarily inflate a deflated ego. It loosens one up and allows one to connect more easily with others and to express feelings such as anger. For adults who grew up in a home that was filled with tension and anxiety, where poor coping skills were modeled, alcohol may be a drug or a self-soothing mechanism.

Children from alcoholic homes often decide to drink at the same age and for the same reasons as do children of nonalcoholic families. They may begin drinking in their early teens to have fun, to fit in with peers, or out of curiosity, experimentation, or defiance. They may learn to drink as a way to escape. However, they drink with an extra belief that "it will never happen to me." They believe that alcoholism is a matter of willpower and that they have seen too many negative aspects of alcohol to ever lose control themselves.[19] They do not understand that they may already have a biological or emotional predisposition to alcoholism.

Ask members if they have questions.

B. *Exercise Four*
    1. Objective: To increase members' awareness of how childhood roles may predispose the individual to alcohol dependency.
    2. Discuss the following question as a full group: How might the overly responsible adult child be vulnerable to dependency on alcohol or other chemicals? The adjuster? The placater?
    3. Include the following points in the discussion:
       a. *The overachiever*: If your role as an adult child is that of the overachiever, you have many positive reinforcers to drink. Drinking may be the only way that you can loosen up and allow yourself not to be in total control. Alcohol, because it breaks down inhibitions, allows you to relax and to appear less serious, less tense, and more playful. It may help you to become a better listener, which in turn makes people warm up to you and feel more connected with you.* When you drink, you become more open about your feelings and more vulnerable, which results in other people responding more positively to you. You have a feeling of belonging and wholeness. However, to sustain these feelings you must continue to drink during social occasions. Although this pattern does not make you an alcoholic, these positive reinforcers can predispose you to a psychological dependency on alcohol.[20]
       b. *The adjuster*: Adjusters see themselves as powerless and repress their anger at others in order to be able to adjust to a situation. Alcohol gives these people a false sense of power.

If you are an adjuster, you may challenge authority or get in touch with your own anger when you drink. The power that you experience while drinking makes you feel less inadequate. You may see more options when you drink and be able to make decisions. It may be easier for you to get in touch with your real feelings and to express them when you are drinking. You may be less concerned about pleasing others when you are drinking. However, in order to maintain this sense of power and choice, you must continue to drink, which sets you up for a dependency on alcohol. The good feelings that you experience while drinking do not occur without the use of alcohol.[21]

    c. Placaters always focus on the needs of others. Alcohol allows placaters to feel less guilty about meeting their own needs. It allows them to talk more freely about themselves and to have a greater sense of self-worth and feeling of wholeness. If you are a placater, you may become more assertive or even express anger when you drink. Drinking creates positive feelings about yourself and the sense that you, too, are entitled to receive from others. However, you need to continue to drink in order to sustain these feelings. This does not make you an alcoholic, but sets you up for psychological dependency.[22]

    d. The scapegoat may drink as a way of being accepted by marginally functioning peers who also drink. As an adult, the scapegoat may drink to deal with his or her sense of being a loser and to temporarily forget feelings of low self-worth.

  4. Ask members if they have questions.

C. *Mini-Lecture: Adult Relationships**
What children learn in their homes, they take with them into adulthood. Life doesn't change for these people emotionally just because they leave the alcoholic family system. The system and its rules, as well as the issues of that system, are taken with the children when they leave the family. As adult children of alcoholics, we either become alcoholics, marry them, or both, or find another compulsive personality to meet our needs.

Therefore, when adult children of alcoholics marry, they usually choose a mate who was also raised in an alcoholic home, an alcoholic, a workaholic, or someone with a compulsive personality. Having grown up in a home in which emotional support, communication, and intimacy were lacking, adult children marry persons who also have difficulty with communication and intimacy.

The adult child does not feel safe in close relationships and consequently feels distant from others.

"When I enter into interpersonal relationships, I need to find a person who will give me some distance, who isn't going to want to get too close to me. When you get too close to me, you want more from me than I can give and I feel scared. I don't understand it, but I feel scared. I don't know how to talk honestly, so I don't want someone who talks honestly. I don't know how to talk about my feelings, so I want to find you, who doesn't want to talk openly about feelings. I want someone who will also not talk about problems, who will minimize them and pretend they're not there."

People tend to gravitate in relationships toward that which feels comfortable and familiar. If you grow up in a home in which feelings are not positively expressed, communication is poor, and intimacy does not exist, you do not learn how to relate to others in positive, healthy ways. As adult children of alcoholics, you might have longed for more closeness or intimacy, and you also may have feared it because you really do not know how to behave in intimate relationships. If you were an overly responsible child, you may marry an alcoholic and take care of him or her just as you did when you were a child. If you were an adjuster, you will accommodate the alcoholic's behavior. If you marry a compulsive personality, such as a workaholic, this person will not be there for you when you need him or her. This person will always put his or her compulsion first (be it alcohol or work) and thus avoid emotional intimacy.

Although children of alcoholics tend to marry alcoholics or other compulsive personalities, they rarely enter the marriage with this knowledge. They may compare their spouse's drinking with their own parent's drinking patterns and be unable to identify the similarities, perhaps because the illness is at an early stage or is manifesting itself somewhat differently from the way it did with their own parents. For example, "John never got violent when he drank, as my father did." Of course, one reason for not seeing the handwriting on the wall is denial, which allows people not to see that which is too painful for them to see and allows them to rationalize or minimize a problem.

D. *Mini-Lecture: Risk of Alcoholism**

Alcoholism is a family illness that is often passed from one generation to the next. Fifty percent of all alcoholics have at least one alcoholic parent. Obviously, not all children who grow up in alcoholic homes become alcoholics themselves. However, alcoholism may skip a generation and reappear in the children of adult children of alcoholics, who do not drink themselves.

When adult children leave home, unless they have been involved in a therapeutic process, they carry their emotional baggage with them. If they do not learn how to communicate and to express feelings instead of stuffing them, they will pass their poor communication skills on to their own children. If the person finds it difficult to express anger, it will be difficult for his or her children to understand or be comfortable with their own anger. Unless the adult child is involved in a therapeutic process, he or she will have the same emotional issues as the alcoholic, that is, viewing everything in terms of black and white; being rigid and controlling; not talking, feeling, or trusting; and taking responsibility for everyone but him- or herself. Except for the excessive drinking, all the other dysfunctional ways of interacting are modeled in the home and contribute to the family's sense of isolation, powerlessness, and low self-esteem.

Individuals who are raised in an alcoholic family also develop alcoholic attitudes and personality traits.[23]
- Excessive dependency
- Inability to express emotions
- Low frustration tolerance
- Emotional immaturity
- High level of anxiety in interpersonal relationships
- Low self-esteem
- Grandiosity
- Feelings of isolation
- Perfectionism
- Ambivalence toward authority
- Guilt
- Not taking responsibility for oneself or one's behavior

These qualities are transmitted to and shared by family members.

REFERENCES

1. Charles Deutsch, *Broken Bottles, Broken Dreams* (New York: Teachers College Press, 1982), p. 71.
2. Ibid., p. 73.
3. Ibid., p. 72–73.
4. Ibid., p. 73–74.
5. Claudia Black, *It Will Never Happen to Me!* (Denver: ACT, 1982), p. 24.
6. Ibid.
7. Black, *It Will Never Happen to Me!*, pp. 24–25.
8. Ibid., p. 21.
9. Ibid., p. 60.
10. Ibid.
11. Ibid., p. 61.
12. Ibid.
13. Ibid., pp. 129–30.
14. Ibid., p. 130.
15. Ibid., pp. 131–32.
16. Janet Geringer Woititz, *Adult Children of Alcoholics* (Pompano Beach, Fla.: Health Communications, 1983), p. 103.
17. Black, *It Will Never Happen to Me!*, p. 4.
18. Woititz, *Adult Children of Alcoholics*, p. 103.
19. Black, *It Will Never Happen to Me!*, p. 53.
20. Ibid., p. 56.
21. Ibid., pp. 18–19.
22. Ibid., p. 61.
23. Woititz, *Adult Children of Alcoholics*, p. 103.

HANDOUT—SESSION 5

Characteristics of the Alcoholic Personality
That Are Shared by Adult Children of Alcoholics**

Alcoholic
- excessive dependency
- inability to express emotions
- low frustration tolerance
- emotional immaturity
- high level of anxiety in interpersonal relationships
- low self-esteem
- grandiosity
- feelings of isolation
- perfectionism
- ambivalence toward authority
- guilt
- dependency
- denial
- protectiveness, pity, and concern for the drinker
- self-absorptive activities
- obsession, continual worry
- fear
- lying
- false hope, disappointment, euphoria
- confusion
- sexual problems
- anger
- lethargy, hopelessness, self-pity, remorse, despair

Thus adult children of alcoholic parents are the products of their environment.

**Adapted from Janet Geringer Woititz, *Adult Children of Alcoholics* (Pompano Beach, Fla.: Health Communications, 1983), p. 105. Used with permission.

HANDOUT—SESSION 5

Positive Messages for
Adult Children of Alcoholics**

- My needs are important.
- It is OK to put my own well-being first.
- I don't have to take care of everyone else.
- Others can lend support to those who need it when I am not willing to be available.
- I have choices about how I respond to people.
- I'm not guilty because others feel bad.
- I deserve to be given a thank-you.
- I can enjoy receiving praise.

**Claudia Black, *It Will Never Happen to Me!* (Denver: ACT, 1981), p. 130. Used with permission.

SESSION 6

OBJECTIVE: To increase members' awareness of adult-child issues such as feeling isolated and afraid of people, feeling different from other people, overreacting to changes over which they have no control, fear of angry people and any personal criticism, difficulties handling conflict, and addiction to negative excitement.

I. OPENING THE SESSION

A. Review of Session 5: Ask members if they wish to comment on previous session.

B. Brief overview of Session 6.

II. ADULT-CHILD ISSUES

A. *Mini-Lecture: Introduction to Issues*
Because of the unspoken rules in an alcoholic family—don't talk, don't feel, don't trust—as well as the effects of your role in the family, you are left with many unresolved issues that continue to affect you as an adult.[1] These issues include difficulties with communication, trust, and establishing intimate relationships. As adult children, you find it difficult to resolve conflict. You may be addicted to excitement and impulsive behavior. You have low self-esteem and fear abandonment and loss of control. Many of you do not have a clear idea as to what constitutes normal behavior. These and other issues will be covered in depth in the following sessions.

B. *Mini-Lecture: Feeling Isolated and Afraid of People*
As children, you did not have your own dependency needs met and did not have parents who nurtured and cared for you in a consistent fashion. Because you were not able to depend on others either to validate your needs or feelings or to be there for you emotionally or physically, you withdrew from those around you. You learned not to trust others and relied more heavily on yourself. Initially, this

behavior protected you. Now that you are adults, however, this behavior isolates you from others. As children you learned that the only person you could count on was yourself. You found it difficult to view adults as viable resources.*

As children, you were not encouraged to talk about parental alcoholism within or outside the family. You felt no one would understand or be willing to listen. Your feelings of isolation as a child make it difficult for you to connect with others as an adult. As a child and now as an adult, you longed for connection. However, to connect with others, one must be in touch with one's own feelings, know how to talk about them, and trust others enough to become vulnerable. In order to overcome their sense of isolation, adult children must learn how to talk, how to feel, and how to trust. The adult child must risk sharing with others and letting others get to know him or her; not risking leaves one isolated and lonely.[2] You may have no frame of reference for what is permissible for you to say or feel. In a more healthy home, feelings are not repressed all the time, nor do people feel that they must always walk on eggshells.[3]

In working toward recovery, it is probably more helpful to think in terms of healthy and unhealthy rather than normal and abnormal. For example, Is this a healthy thing to do? Is this a healthy way to act? Is this a healthy way to meet my needs? to resolve problems? to deal with conflict? The behavior and personal interactions that you saw modeled as a child were unhealthy.

Adult children of alcoholics feel that they are different from other people and often find it difficult to relate to others because they are afraid that people will see them as different. The adult child's sense of isolation and inability to connect with people through talking and sharing feeds his or her sense of being different. Feeling different is something that adult children have experienced since early childhood. Other children were carefree and cared for. You, however, were always concerned about what was going on at home and thus could never feel completely comfortable while playing with other children. Home problems hovered like a cloud over everything in your life.[4]

Because you did not learn how to talk about feelings or yourself, you did not develop the social skills necessary to feel comfortable or part of a group. You felt isolated and that you had to guard the family secret.[5] As an adult, you now assume that if people really knew about you and your past, they would not like you or want to know you. Because your past is unacceptable to you, you fear rejection from others. Even in a group of other adult children, you may feel different. This feeling of being unacceptable makes you uncomfortable in social situations. Adult children "assume that in any group of people everyone else feels comfortable and they are the only ones who feel awkward." They do not realize that others struggle with this issue as well.[6]

Ask members if they have questions.

C. *Exercise One*
 1. Objective: To help members get in touch with their feelings of isolation as a child and as an adult.
 2. Break into dyads.
 3. Ask members the following question: Do you remember feeling isolated as a child? Do you still feel isolated as an adult?
 4. Discuss as a full group; include the following points.
  After you take the risk of sharing your experiences with other individuals from a similar background, you will begin to understand that although you are unique as a person, you are not that different from others.[7] In a group such as Adult Children of Alcoholics, you can risk letting individuals know who you are while you get to know yourself better. You begin to relate and identify with other people, which diminishes feelings of being different and isolated.

D. *Mini-Lecture: Overreacting to Changes
 Over Which You Have No Control*
 Growing up in an alcoholic home, you were unable to control the circumstances of your life.[8] You could not control what happened to you, although you may have tried to do so through the family role that you assumed. The alcoholic's disease and the situation at home got progressively worse. The drinking, the family crises, and the emotional outbursts became more and more out of control, which is frightening to a child of any age.

As a child, you were also victimized by your parent's inconsistency and undependability. You never knew whether the alcoholic would let you down or whether he or she would be abusive or loving. Moreover, you may also have been overly controlled as a child as a result of your parent's rigidity and their standards of perfection.

As a result, it became increasingly important for you to battle these feelings of being out of control by taking control of your environment, a behavior that is carried into adulthood. In fact, loss of control and fear of abandonment are the two biggest fears of adult children of alcoholics.*

Because of this constant need to be in control, adult children of alcoholics are often accused of being rigid and controlling, of having to have things their own way, of being inflexible, and of lacking spontaneity. Although this accusation may be well founded, such behavior is not the result of selfishness or needing to have everything one's own way. Rather, it comes from the fear that if you are not in total control, that if a change is made and you don't have a say in it, you will lose total control of your life. This is definitely an overreaction. Such overreactions are usually caused by something in one's past experience. An overreaction is not caused by the incident itself, but rather by all the past feelings of hurt and disappointment. Overreaction results from one's own history.[9] You may overreact to something as small as friends changing their plans with you at the last minute or canceling their plans to see you. Or you may find yourself going from feeling irritated to enraged to panic stricken if a friend is more than five to ten minutes late meeting you. Minor changes such as these trigger your fear of abandonment and losing control.

Adult children are not the only people who feel hurt or are disappointed when plans are changed at the last minute or when things do not work out the way they hoped. However, whereas someone else might feel hurt or let down, the adult child feels devastated, abandoned, out of control, or even paranoid about the other person's motives. Your overreaction is caused by all the past feelings of hurt and disappointment at all the other plans that were never carried out due to your mother's or father's drinking. If you begin to ask yourself whether a situation warranted your reacting to it as strongly as you did, you can begin to identify when you are overreacting and begin to realize that many feelings are related to your past and not to the present. Although you may still feel hurt or disappointment, you do not have to let it devastate your whole being.[10]

Ask members if they have any questions.

E. *Exercise Two*
    1. Objective: To increase members' awareness of how they feel

when they are not in control of a situation or when plans are changed unexpectedly.

2. Break into dyads.
3. Ask members the following questions: How do you feel when you are not in control of a situation? What feelings get stirred up? How do you feel when others unexpectedly change their plans? Did this often happen to you when you were a child?
4. Discuss as a full group.

F. *Mini-Lecture: Anger and Criticism*
Adult children of alcoholics are frightened by angry people and by any personal criticism. They fear criticism and judgment, yet are critical and judgmental of others. They judge themselves harshly and without mercy and have a very low sense of self-esteem. Having grown up in a home environment in which anger was expressed explosively or abusively, you have learned to fear people who are angry or critical. You equate anger with loss of control, with being lashed out at, or with being victimized unfairly and irrationally. You also fear personal criticism because as a child you could never meet the alcoholic's standards of perfection. Criticism at home was rarely constructive and was often humiliating, demeaning, or in the form of a personal attack.

Although you have learned to fear criticism, you have also become highly critical of both yourself and others. Having been judged against perfectionistic standards, you internalized your parents' standards and became quite judgmental of yourself and others. Adult children of alcoholics tend to be very hard on themselves. They blame themselves for the mistakes they make. When things go wrong, they view it as their fault. At the same time, they find it difficult to give themselves credit for things they do well.

In an attempt to avoid anger and criticism, many of you have sought approval from others and have lost your identity in the process. You did everything you could not to anger the alcoholic. Consequently, as adults you find it difficult to stand up for yourself and to say no to others. You don't feel confident that people will like you for who you are but only for what you do.

Ask members if they have questions.

G. *Exercise Three*
1. Objective: To increase members' awareness of their fear of angry

and critical people as well as of their need for approval.

2. Break into dyads to discuss the following questions: Are you afraid of being the target of anger or criticism? Does this result in your feeling defensive when you are criticized? Do you find yourself doing whatever you can do to avoid disapproval or to gain approval from others? Do you see yourself as needing to be a people pleaser?

3. Discuss as a full group.

H. *Mini-Lecture: Dealing with Conflict*

"I avoid conflict or aggravate it. Rarely do I deal with it."

Most adult children avoid conflict at all costs. If something bothers them, they will usually suppress it rather than confront the other person. Their resentment accumulates until it is finally expressed explosively, either verbally or physically, which only serves to aggravate the conflict.

As adult children of alcoholics, you had no strong models for positive conflict resolution. You rarely saw two adults sit down to discuss a problem in its early, middle, or late stages. The adults around you did not handle their anger early on when it was manageable. You had no model for working out compromises. Someone won or someone lost, all or nothing, win or lose, black or white. As adult children, you must learn how to sit down and discuss what is bothering you in a calm and rational manner. This is a difficult task, especially if you feel powerless, or if no one is willing to listen or care.

Some adult children try to avoid conflict by saying yes when they want to say no. If you say yes when you want to say no, you may avoid an immediate confrontation, but not the conflict. The conflict is internalized. It is a myth to think that you can avoid conflict by avoiding confrontation.

I. *Exercise Four*
1. Objective: To increase members' awareness of how they tend to avoid conflict or aggravate it.
2. Break into dyads and ask the following questions: How do you deal with conflict? Do you tend to avoid it? If so, how? Do you tend to aggravate it? If so, how?
3. Discuss as a group.

J. *Mini-Lecture: Addiction to Crisis and Negative Excitement*

Adult children of alcoholics, who grew up in homes in which crisis, chaos, and physical or verbal abuse were prevalent and in which emotions were expressed in volatile or violent ways, often become addicted to negative excitement and crises. Even if your childhood home was not as extreme as that described above, you still would have been affected by the inconsistency of the alcoholic's behavior, by not knowing what to expect or how you would be treated.

In your alcoholic home, the kind of excitement that existed was not the excitement of looking forward to a family picnic or going to the movies. The excitement that was present was that of crisis and unpredictability. You never knew if your parent would come home drunk or if he or she would already be drinking when you got home from school. You lived with the negative excitement of not knowing whether your parents would show up at the school play or P.T.A. meeting, of being afraid in the car while your parent drove drunk, of not knowing whether your parent's drinking would result in another fight or in physical or verbal abuse.

As adult children, you manifest your addiction to excitement in various ways. Often, your behavior is compulsive. You may look for immediate forms of gratification because they are the most rewarding. You may spend money impulsively or gamble compulsively, and thus create financial crises for yourself. You may act impulsively when it comes to sex. You may procrastinate and thus create crises in meeting deadlines, or you may overextend yourself on the job or socially. You may choose friends or mates who are undependable or who are also crisis oriented because they feed your addiction to negative excitement. In so doing, you recreate old feelings of excitement when you were a child in an alcoholic home. This excitement acts as a drug, much as alcohol does for the alcoholic, and allows you not to experience your feelings of emptiness, loneliness, fear, or depression.

K. *Exercise Five*
1. Objective: To increase members' awareness of how they may be addicted to excitement.
2. Ask the group the following question: What are the things you do to generate negative excitement in your life?
3. Discuss as a group.

Ask members if they wish to ask questions.

REFERENCES

1. Claudia Black, *It Will Never Happen to Me!* (Denver: ACT, 1982), pp. 33–49
2. Janet Geringer Woititz, *Adult Children of Alcoholics* (Pompano Beach, Fla.: Health Communications, 1983), p. 81.
3. Ibid., p. 28.
4. Ibid., pp. 48–49.
5. Ibid., p. 49.
6. Ibid., p. 48.
7. Ibid., p. 81.
8. Ibid., p. 46.
9. Ibid., pp. 46–47.
10. Ibid., p. 78.

HANDOUT—SESSION 6

Adult-Child Issues:
The Problem and the Solution

Preamble: Adult Children of Alcoholics (ACOA) is an anonymous fellowship of men and women who wish to heal themselves and become aware of self-destructive patterns through sharing experiences, strengths, and hope with one another.

Adult Children of Alcoholics do not wish to blame, but rather to understand, the family disease concept of alcoholism, so we can become free to grow and accept responsibility for our own lives.

Adult Children of Alcoholics is self-supporting through our own voluntary contributions. We are not allied with any sect, denomination, politics, organization, or institution; do not wish to engage in any controversy; neither endorse nor oppose any causes.

Our primary purpose is to heal through knowledge and help other children of alcoholics let go of the pain of yesterday and, through living today, gain hope for tomorrow.

The Problem: We seem to have several characteristics in common as a result of having been brought up in an alcoholic household.

- We have become isolated and afraid of people and authority figures.
- We became approval seekers and lost our identity in the process.
- We are frightened by angry people and any personal criticism.
- We either become alcoholics, marry them, or both, or find another compulsive personality—such as a workaholic—to fill our sick abandonment needs.
- We live life from the viewpoint of victims and are attracted by that weakness in our love, friendship, and career relationships.
- We have an overdeveloped sense of responsibility, and it is

easier for us to be concerned with others rather than ourselves. This enables us not to look too closely at our faults or to take responsibility for ourselves.

- We feel guilty when we stand up for ourselves instead of giving in to others.
- We become addicted to excitement.
- We confuse love and pity and tend to "love" people we can "pity" and "rescue."
- We have "stuffed" our feelings from our traumatic childhoods and have lost the ability to feel or express our feelings because it hurts so much. This includes good feelings such as joy and happiness. Being out of touch with our feelings is one of our basic forms of denial.
- We judge ourselves harshly and have a very low sense of self-esteem.
- We are dependent personalities and are terrified of abandonment and will do anything to hold on to a relationship in order not to experience painful abandonment feelings. We receive this from living with sick people who were never there for us emotionally.
- Alcoholism is a family disease. We became para-alcoholics and took on the characteristics of the disease even if we did not drink.
- Para-alcoholics are reactors rather than actors.

The Solution: By attending recovery meetings on a regular basis, we learn that we can live our lives in a more meaningful manner. We learn to change our attitudes, patterns, and habits and find serenity and even happiness.

- Alcoholism is a disease that affects our mental, physical, and spiritual lives. Our parents were victims of this disease, which ends in insanity, death, or, hopefully, recovery. Learning about and understanding the disease is the beginning of the gift of forgiveness.
- We learn the three Cs—we didn't cause it, we can't control it and we can't cure it.
- We learn to focus on ourselves and to be good to ourselves.
- We learn to detach with love and to give ourselves and others "tough love."
- We use the recovery slogans "Let Go and Let God," "Easy Does It," "One Day at a Time," "Keep It Simple," "Live and Let Live." Using these slogans helps us to lead our daily lives in a new way.

- We learn to feel, to accept, and to express our feelings as well as to build self-esteem.
- Through working with the Twelve Steps, we learn to accept the disease and realize that our lives have become unmanageable and that we are powerless over the disease and the alcoholic. As we become willing to admit our defects and our sick thinking, we are able to change our attitudes and to turn our reactions into actions. By working within the program and admitting that we are powerless, we come to eventually believe in the spirituality of the program, that there is a solution other than ourselves, that there is a higher power—God, as we understand Him. By sharing our experience, relating to others, welcoming newcomers, and serving our group, we build self-esteem.
- We learn to love ourselves. In this way we are able to love others in a healthy way.
- We have telephone therapy with people with whom we relate. This helps at all times—not just when problems arise.
- By applying the Serenity Prayer to our daily lives, we begin to change the sick attitudes we acquired in childhood.
- We suggest regular attendance at AA or Al-Anon meetings.

Additional Adult-Child Issues

1. I guess at what normal is.
2. I have difficulty following projects through from beginning to end.
3. I lie when it would be just as easy to tell the truth.
4. I judge myself without mercy.
5. I have difficulty having fun.
6. I take myself very seriously.
7. I have difficulty with intimate relationships.
8. I overreact to changes over which I have no control.
9. I feel different from other people.
10. I constantly seek approval and affirmation.
11. I am either super responsible or super irresponsible.
12. I am extremely loyal even in the face of evidence that the loyalty is undeserved.
13. I look for immediate as opposed to deferred gratification.
14. I lock myself into a course of action without giving serious consideration to alternative behaviors or possible consequences.

15. I seek tension and crisis and then complain about the results.
16. I avoid conflict or aggravate it; rarely do I deal with it.
17. I fear rejection and abandonment, yet I reject others.
18. I fear failure, but sabotage my success.
19. I fear criticism and judgment, yet I am critical and judgmental of others.
20. I manage my time poorly and do not set my priorities in a way that works well for me.

In order to change, I cannot use my history as an excuse for continuing my behaviors. I have no regrets for what might have been, because my experiences have shaped my talents as well as my defects of character. It is my responsibility to discover these talents, to build my self-esteem and to repair any damage done. I will allow myself to feel my feelings, to accept them, and will learn to express them appropriately. When I have begun these tasks, I will try to let go of my past and get on with the business of managing my life.

I have survived against impossible odds until today. With the help of God and my friends, I shall survive the next twenty-four hours. I am no longer alone.

Reprinted with permission from "I Am an Adult Who Grew Up in an Alcoholic Family" (Rutherford, N.J.: Thomas W. Perrin, Inc., 1983).

SESSION 7

OBJECTIVES: To help members become more aware of their fear of abandonment, their extreme loyalty (even when evidence suggests that this loyalty is undeserved), their difficulty with intimate relationships, and guidelines for healthy intimate relationships.

I. OPENING THE SESSION

A. Review of Session 6: Ask members if they wish to comment on previous week's session.

B. Brief overview of Session 7.

II. ABANDONMENT ISSUES

A. *Mini-Lecture: Fear of Abandonment*
Issue: We are dependent personalities who are terrified of abandonment and who will do anything to hold onto a relationship in order not to experience painful abandonment feelings. We receive this from living with sick people who were never there for us emotionally.

Adult children of alcoholics are dependent individuals because their early dependency needs were not consistently met in a loving way. As children, you could not depend on adults to give you the emotional or physical support you needed on a regular basis. The alcoholic in your family was preoccupied with his or her drinking. He or she might have been physically absent if most of the drinking was done outside the home or if he or she was a workaholic as well as an alcoholic. If the alcoholic drank at home, he or she would be off in another world or perhaps unsafe to be around.

The nonalcoholic parent, if there was one, was also emotionally unavailable. This parent was largely preoccupied with the drinking of the alcoholic and was often under stress. As a result, you may have been the target for this parent's anger or frustrations, which really should have been directed at the alcoholic. This parent may have been very abrupt with you or perhaps spent very little time with you. The time that was spent together was used to take care of basic needs such as eating, getting you dressed, or putting you to bed, rather than talking to you or playing with you. You felt abandoned by your parents in many ways. You felt alone or isolated in your family, because no one seemed to pay attention to your needs or feelings. You felt as though you had no one to turn to, talk to, trust, or feel close to.[1]

As adult children you must also deal with issues concerning abandonment because of the inconsistency of the alcoholic, who was loving one minute and rejecting the next. This inconsistency, this constant switching from loving to rejecting behavior, or even the consistency of the rejecting behavior, left you with a constant fear of abandonment.[2] To some degree, all children are afraid of abandonment because of their total dependence on adults. However, this fear becomes extreme under the conditions that exist in the alcoholic home.

Fear of abandonment is often the glue that holds many unhappy relationships, friendships, or marriages together for adult children of alcoholics. Even abuse, whether physical or emotional, can be less frightening and less painful to cope with and tolerate than abandonment. As a child, you learned to adjust and cope with the abuse even though you hated it. You coped in order to survive. Abuse was a "known," but abandonment hung like a sword ready to fall. As a child, and now as an adult, you were so afraid that people you loved would leave you that you never stopped to think whether they were really there for you in the first place. Adult children often say that they remain in a marriage because they are afraid of being alone. However, if they are honest and look past their fears, they will realize that they may have felt lonely and alone throughout their marriage.

This terrible feeling of abandonment that adult children experience not only gets in the way of developing relationships, but gets in the way of severing them as well.[3] Adult children often remain in relationships that would be better off dissolved, because they are afraid that there will never again be someone to love or care about them.[4] Willingness to tolerate abusive or unacceptable behavior is very much related to low self-esteem. The two greatest fears of adult children of alcoholics are fear of abandonment and loss of control.*

Ask members if they have questions.

B. *Exercise One*
   1. Objective: To increase members' awareness of abandonment issues.
   2. Break into dyads.
   3. Ask the following questions: Do you remember fearing abandonment as a child? What was the nature of your fears? As an adult, do you still fear that people whom you care about may leave you or stop loving you?
   4. Discuss questions as a group. Include the following points: To many adult children of alcoholics, abandonment feels like the ultimate loss of control. However, if you work on your feelings concerning abandonment so that you are no longer controlled by your fears, you may regain a sense of control over your life. You can begin to make real choices in relationships based on a realistic assessment of whether your needs are being met or whether your relationship is a satisfying one.

C. *Mini-Lecture: Confusing Loyalty with Dependency*
   Issue: Adult children of alcoholics are extremely loyal, even when this loyalty is undeserved.

   "The alcoholic home appears to be a very loyal place where family members hang on long after reason tells them they should leave."[5] The spouse stays with the alcoholic despite the increased ignoring of household responsibilities and the verbal or physical abuse. Loyalty is also demonstrated in the ways that family members cover up for the alcoholic.

   The loyalty that is demonstrated in an alcoholic family is related to the family's fears and insecurities and is not loyalty in the true sense of the word. Spouses often remain with the alcoholic because of their own dependency needs and fear of abandonment. Having witnessed this as children, adult children of alcoholics tend to remain in relationships that are better off dissolved.[6]

   Loyalty is not an admirable trait when it is applied indiscriminately and without judgment. If you are involved with people who do not treat you well, it is important that you rethink your loyalty.[7] Because abandonment is such a major issue for you, you may be tempted to hold onto a relationship with anyone who has gotten to know you a little and has not rejected you, even if this person treats you poorly. In fact, adult children will rationalize this poor treatment by being either overly understanding and finding excuses for unac-

ceptable behavior or by blaming themselves and consequently rein-
forcing their negative self-image.[8]

In rethinking your loyalty, you should ask yourself how you feel
about the person's present behavior toward you. If you start saying
"but," you are no longer dealing with the present, but are fantasizing
about how things used to be or how you hope they will be. During
the initial stages of a relationship, people often treat each other differently from the way they do after a relationship is established. As
adult children, you often blame yourselves when the other person's
behavior changes. All relationships change as people get to know
each other. Relationships become more or less meaningful; people
become more or less considerate. The present is what is real. Is this
relationship best for you at this moment? Fantasizing that things
will be good again, if you can just get through this difficult time, may
not be realistic.[9]

Remember the following:
1. Loyalty, like respect, is not automatic and needs to be earned.
   You have a right to reevaluate a relationship.
2. People who are undeserving of your loyalty are quite often critical and nonsupportive.
3. You do not have to remain in a relationship out of guilt or
   because someone is dependent on you. You have the right to back
   off from a relationship if your needs are not being met, even if the
   other person tries to make you feel guilty.
4. You are not obligated to maintain a relationship because someone
   befriended you. If someone cares about you, it is because you are
   of value and are worth being cared about. Your friendship is a
   gift. If you feel that you owe someone simply because he or she
   befriended you, you are saying that you have no value and that
   you are the only person who stands to gain from this friendship
   because you have nothing to offer others, which simply is not
   true.[10]

Ask members if they have questions.

D. *Exercise Two*
   1. Objective: To have group members examine their tendency to be
      overly loyal to others.
   2. Break into dyads. Ask the following questions: Think of a time
      that a parent, friend, or family member did something that hurt
      you. Did you make an excuse for his or her behavior or blame

80

yourself? Do you do this often? Has this led to your tolerating treatment that you have felt was unacceptable?

3. Discuss as a group. Include the following points:
As adult children of alcoholics, you may not know what a good relationship is like. You may compare your spouse with your alcoholic parent and say, "At least he doesn't beat me and at least he goes to work!" You may not realize that you don't get points for that.[11] You may find that you are developing relationships with people who behave as your parents did. You may be repeating a pattern that is familiar because you have not broken your early ties.[12]

You may find it difficult to let go of relationships because you are afraid that you will not have another opportunity to have a friend, a lover, or a spouse. As you develop new friendships that are healthier, you can begin to let go of the ones that are not good for you. You deserve to be treated with respect and consideration. You must learn to focus on whether your needs are being met by the relationship.[13]

E. *Mini-Lecture: Intimacy*

Issue: Adult children have difficulty with intimate relationships.

If you were raised in a home where you learned the rules don't talk, don't feel, don't trust, you are set up at an early age to have difficulty with intimate relationships as an adult. True intimacy cannot exist without communication, trust, and the expression of needs and feelings. If you do not trust people, how can you let someone get close to you? If you do not trust others, how can you allow yourself to be vulnerable or take risks? How can you let someone know what your needs and feelings are if you do not have the ability to trust or to communicate?*

As adult children, you may desire a healthy intimate relationship, but you may have difficulty because you have no frame of reference for developing such a relationship. As a child, you could not depend on those closest to you to meet your needs, validate you emotionally, or be supportive. You received contradictory messages from your parents, such as "I love you. Go away!"[14]

As children, you did not experience a consistently loving parent–child relationship. Although your parents might have said that they loved you and although you heard and felt those words, you also knew that you were in the way, that you got in your parents' hair, that they often did not have time for you. "I love you. Go away!" is a confusing message. Which part of the message did you believe? If you believed both parts as a child, then people who tell you that they love you, yet push you away, can seem extremely appealing when you are an adult.[15]

As a child you felt loved one day and rejected the next. You carried this feeling with you into adulthood. The fear of being abandoned is a terrible fear. Because love was conditional in your family and was given or taken away at a moment's notice, you lived in constant fear of abandonment. This fear of abandonment keeps you from developing healthy relationships. You do not feel that you can trust people not to hurt you or leave you; consequently, you may keep people at a distance.[16]

This fear may be carried into every aspect of a relationship. All relationships require a great deal of give and take in order to successfully handle differences of opinion and conflicts. Issues of disagreement, anger, and hurt must always be dealt with between couples and friends. According to Woititz, "A minor disagreement gets very big very quickly for adult children of alcoholics, because the issue of being abandoned takes precedence over the original issue."[17] When a problem arises in a relationship, adult children often panic and the problem is never discussed. Adult children often feel so insecure when conflict arises that they may need total reassurance that the other individual still loves them and won't leave them, even if that person may be too angry to give this reassurance, because the actual issue at hand cannot be discussed and dealt with.

Fear of abandonment affects your ability to be confident about yourself in relationships. You may feel that you are unlovable or unworthy of love. You look to others for your sense of self-worth. This gives a lot of power to the other person.[18]

Ask members if they have questions.

F. *Exercise Three*
   1. Objective: To increase members' awareness of their difficulties with intimate relationships.
   2. Discuss the following questions as a group: Do you find it difficult to get close to people or to let others get close to you? What

do you think gets in the way of forming close friendships or relationships?

- Difficulties concerning trust?
- Poor communication?
- Difficulty letting others know what your needs are?
- Difficulty resolving conflict?
- Fear of abandonment?
- Fear of losing control?
- Fear of vulnerability?

3. Include the following points in your discussion:
    Your overwhelming fear of abandonment and rejection prevents any ease in the process of developing healthy relationships. As adult children you also bring a sense of urgency to relationships, as though this relationship is the only one you will ever have. Such behavior puts pressure on a relationship and makes it difficult for the relationship to evolve slowly. People need time to get to know each other, to learn about each other's feelings and attitudes. Healthy relationships take time to develop.[19]

    Ingredients necessary for a healthy relationship include the following:[20]

vulnerability	consideration
trust	honesty
understanding	communication
compassion	compromise
acceptance	compatibility
respect	integrity

    The degree to which these ingredients are present will determine the degree of intimacy that will exist in the relationship. The absence of one or more of these ingredients will create a void in the relationship.[21]

    Ask members if they have questions.

REFERENCES

1. Claudia Black, *It Will Never Happen to Me!* (Denver: ACT, 1981), pp. 43–44.
2. Janet Geringer Woititz, *Adult Children of Alcoholics* (Pompano Beach, Fla.: Health Communications, 1983), p. 41.
3. Ibid., p. 43.
4. Ibid., p. 90.

5. Woititz, *Adult Children of Alcoholics*, p. 51.
6. Ibid., p. 51.
7. Ibid., pp. 87–88.
8. Ibid., pp. 51–52.
9. Ibid., p. 90.
10. Ibid., pp. 87–91.
11. Janet Woititz, "Intimate Relationships and Adult Children of Alcoholics," audiotape from the set *Families and Alcoholism* (Indianapolis: Access, 1983).
12. Woititz, *Adult Children of Alcoholics*, p. 89.
13. Ibid., pp. 90–91.
14. Ibid., p. 41.
15. Ibid., p. 19.
16. Ibid., pp. 41–43.
17. Ibid., p. 43.
18. Ibid., p. 44.
19. Ibid., pp. 43–45.
20. Ibid., pp. 71–72.
21. Ibid., p. 72.

HANDOUT— SESSION 7

Ingredients of a Healthy Intimate Relationship

Vulnerability: To what degree am I willing to let down my barriers? To what degree am I willing to allow the other person to affect my feelings?

Understanding: Do I understand the other person? Do I understand what the person means by what he or she says or does?

Empathy: To what degree am I able to allow myself to feel what he or she feels?

Compassion: Do I have a genuine concern for the issues that cause the other person concern?

Respect: Do I treat the other person as if he or she is of value?

Trust: To what degree and on what levels am I willing to let the other person gain access to the things about me that I don't want everybody to know?

Acceptance: Am I O.K. the way I am? Can I accept my partner the way he or she is?

Honesty: Is this relationship built on truth or are there games involved?

Communication: Are we able to talk freely about issues that are important in the relationship? Do we know how to do it so we are understood and the relationship goes forward because of the sharing?

Compatibility: To what degree do we like and dislike the same things? To what degree does it matter if we differ in certain attitudes and beliefs?

Personal Integrity: To what degree am I able to maintain myself as well as offer myself to the other person?

Consideration: Am I mindful of the other person's needs as well as my own?

Reprinted with permission from Janet Geringer Woititz, *Adult Children of Alcoholics* (Pompano Beach, Fla.: Health Communications, 1983), pp. 70–72.

85

SESSION 8

OBJECTIVES: To increase members' awareness of the difficulties they experience with impulse control. To educate group members about individual and group therapy for adult children of alcoholics.

I. OPENING THE SESSION

A. Review of Session 7: Ask members if they wish to comment on the previous week's session.

B. Brief overview of Session 8.

II. ADULT CHILDREN OF ALCOHOLICS AND IMPULSIVITY

A. *Mini-Lecture: Impulsiveness*[1]
Adult children of alcoholics are impulsive. They tend to commit themselves to a course of action without giving serious consideration to alternative behaviors or possible consequences.

Impulsiveness is a very childlike quality. Children are generally very impulsive, but they receive help from their parents in controlling their impulsiveness. Good parents set limits, say no, or use discipline to deal with the child's impulsive behavior. However, children who grow up in alcoholic homes do not receive consistent parenting, limit setting, or discipline. Also, children of alcoholics may sometimes take on the role of parent. People who do not go through a particular developmental stage quite often make up for it at another stage in life. Impulsive behavior in adulthood may be a reaction to a developmental stage that was skipped during childhood.

Impulsive behavior is behavior that is geared to the present without any consideration of past or future consequences. In some ways, such behavior is not unlike that of a two-year-old who has to have what he or she wants when he or she wants it. However, unlike two-year-olds, adults are held responsible for their behavior. Your sense of urgency comes from the feeling that if you do not do something immediately, you will not get a second chance. As a child, if you did not get what you asked for at that very moment, that was the end of it. Promises were always broken. Thus adult children of alcoholics tend to look for immediate as opposed to delayed gratification, which makes it very difficult to plan for the future.

Impulsive behavior is behavior over which you have lost control. Impulsivity leads to confusion, self-loathing, loss of control over your environment, and results in your judging yourself harshly and without mercy. Impulsive behavior often induces a crisis. Thus the light at the end of your tunnel vision may be the head lamp of an oncoming train. By being so determined to do what you want to do, despite the reactions of others, you may find yourself in many embarrassing or outrageous situations. Your behavior may not be that different from that of the alcoholic, your parental role model. Although you may end up being very concerned about your behavior, you must spend a lot of time and energy extricating yourself from the mess you have created. This behavior can be extremely self-defeating.

As adult children, you may do things such as quit your job even if you have no other means of support. You may marry someone without really getting to know that person. You may drop out of school or overeat.

Although not all impulsive decisions are bad, alternatives and consequences should always be considered. You must think about whether you will be comfortable with your decision in the long run so that you do not end up saying, "I wish I hadn't acted so rashly."

You should also consider others who will be affected by your rash behavior. Quitting your job when you are the sole supporter of dependent children may not be a good idea. The problem with immediate gratification is not how it feels. It feels great at the moment. The problem is its later effects on your life.

Some adult children may use impulsive behavior as a self-soothing mechanism. They may spend money when they feel low, drink when they are depressed, or work to forget problems. To break such habits, always stop to consider the possible consequences of your behavior. Ask yourself, "Will I get caught?" If spending money will create financial problems, if eating will result in weight gain, or if drinking will result in erratic behavior, the answer is yes, you will get caught. Then ask yourself if the problems that you will experience will be worth it. Work on freeing yourself of the necessity of acting out your impulses. Doing so will put you back in charge of your life.

B. *Exercise One*
   1. Objective: To increase members' awareness of their difficulties with controlling impulsive behavior.
   2. Ask group to break into dyads to discuss the following questions: Think of a situation in which you acted impulsively, in which you locked yourself into a course of action without considering the consequences. What happened? Did you regret it later? How might you have handled this situation differently with the benefit of hindsight?
   3. Discuss as a group.

III. TREATMENT FOR ADULT CHILDREN OF ALCOHOLICS

A. *Mini-Lecture: Individual Treatment*
   Just as the alcoholic suffers from the disease of alcoholism and needs to be treated for that disease, adult children of alcoholics need to be treated for their own disease, that of codependency. Like alcoholism, codependency is a progressive illness characterized by obsessive thinking and compulsive behavior. Codependents may suffer from relationship addiction or addictions to work, sports, spending, prescription or nonprescription drugs, or alcohol. Codependents suffer from low self-esteem and rely on people, places, and things outside of them for their sense of self-esteem. They depend on others to love and take care of them so they won't have to learn how to love and take care of themselves. Codependents often suffer from stress-related illnesses that are progressive and may eventually be fatal. They tend to internalize stress and "stuff" their resentments so that they can continue to remain and function in dysfunctional and stressful situations or relationships in which their needs are not met.

   In order to recover from their disease of codependency, adult children of alcoholics must deal with some very specific issues in treatment. If you are interested in counseling, it is very important to seek out a professional who is familiar with the issues of adult children of alcoholics, the disease of codependency, as well as with alcoholic family systems in general. An informed therapist would focus on appropriate issues, which are some of the same issues that are dealt with in the self-help program for Adult Children of Alcoholics (ACOA).

   It may be necessary for a therapist to tell you why it is so difficult for you to talk about your feelings and issues before you are able to talk about them. As adult children, many of you are scared to death of your feelings because you equate emotional expression with loss of control or with out-of-control behavior. Your therapist may need to tell you what you experienced and felt as a child in an alcoholic home. You have probably repressed much of what happened to you as a child because it was too traumatic or painful to remember. Many adult children suffer from emotional blackouts and have forgotten huge chunks of their pasts, primarily that which relates to their early childhood.

An essential part of emotional recovery is to reexperience the early pain, sadness, fear, anger, and guilt in a therapeutic environment so that you can let go of it. Otherwise, the repressed emotional pain of the individual continues to affect and distort his or her life. Facing one's pain directly makes it unnecessary to use drugs, alcohol, or crisis situations as avoidance measures. A good therapist will help you connect your past with your present so that you can understand how your current ways of functioning, feeling, and responding are rooted in what you learned as a child in your home.*

To break old patterns of relating, interacting, and reacting, you must first identify the patterns and understand their origin. You must learn that you have the ability to make choices. You can learn to live your life differently by first increasing your awareness of why you behave the way you do. However, to achieve recovery, insight is not enough. One must be in therapy that is experiential as well as insight oriented, therapy geared toward "healing the child within." A good therapist will help you to regress into the pain of the hurt child that is still inside you and will be a witness to your pain. As children, your pain was invisible to your parents, who were so involved in themselves and their own pain that they did not want to see yours. In order to heal, you need to feel again the pain that you felt as a child, but this time in a therapeutic environment, where you do not feel the pain all alone and where soothing and comfort are provided for your pain. Such an atmosphere allows you to finally release the pain of the past, which is what recovery is all about.

During therapy you must learn that the defenses and roles that helped you survive the chaos of the alcoholic home as children now work against you and isolate you as adults. You must face your fear of abandonment, your overreactions to situations in which you are not in control, your low self-esteem, and your difficulties with intimate relationships.

In addition to being treated individually in therapy, it is essential that you attend one or two ACOA meetings each week. Doing so helps reinforce your individual treatment and puts you in touch with feelings and experiences that can be explored in depth during individual therapy. The experience of being listened to, supported, accepted, validated, and cared about in individual therapy is magnified and multiplied by the many people at ACOA program meetings. Feelings of isolation are thus diminished. Involvement in therapy is not enough to achieve recovery. Individuals must also participate in a twelve-step recovery program such as ACOA, in which issues of trust and low self-esteem can be worked on and healed in a group situation. It is essential that we be in a healing group experience, because for most of us our first group experience, our family of origin, was not a good one.

Ask members if they have questions.

B. *Mini-Lecture: Group Therapy*
Some leading professionals who treat adult children of alcoholics view group therapy as the treatment of choice. They feel that sharing one's experiences and feelings in a group greatly decreases the sense of isolation, of being different, of being crazy. It helps adult children feel validated and accepted for who they are. Groups multiply the sense of support and further break down feelings of isolation. It is important for you as adult children to learn that it is all right to talk about what went on in your homes, not just to one person but to other people, that doing so is not a betrayal of your parents, but is an important part of recovery. Group work is a good way to get beyond the rules of the alcoholic family: don't talk, don't feel, don't trust. In a group, you receive permission to talk and see and hear others talking. You learn how to feel in a group because hearing others share their feelings or relay painful experiences that you can identify with helps put you in touch with your own feelings. You learn to "unstuff" the feelings of your traumatic childhood and have those feelings validated by the group. You learn to trust in the group because the environment is safe and conducive to trust. Confidentiality is emphasized. Even more important, through the group you experience what it is like to be accepted and supported instead of criticized and attacked. This supportiveness and validation is provided in a consistent and caring way.

Groups are a powerful vehicle for getting in touch with one's feelings. Many alcohol-treatment facilities offer group treatment on an inpatient basis for adult children of alcoholics or other family members to work on codependency issues. Such programs help individuals to reexperience early emotional trauma in a safe place where they can receive comfort and support for their pain, so they can let go of it. Recovery is about letting go of the pain of the past, so one can be free of it today.

Group therapy also helps adult children to learn how to connect with other people. It teaches them how to listen and how to talk. It gives individuals a sense of hope and of not being alone. As the adult child sees other group members make progress, he or she finds reason to hope for him- or herself.

Ask members if they have questions.

C. *Mini-Lecture: Adult Children Who Are Active Alcoholics or Chemically Dependent*
The following question has been asked: If a person is an active alcoholic or substance abuser and if he or she is also an adult child of an alcoholic, should this person be in treatment for adult-child issues or in the ACOA program? The answer is no. If you are using alcohol or drugs addictively, you cannot make any lasting gains or progress in treatment. You must first arrest your disease of chemical dependency before addressing codependency issues. Although you may initially have tried to medicate yourself with alcohol and drugs for your disease of codependency, in order to recover, your alcoholism must be treated as the primary disease before your issues as an adult child and as a codependent can be addressed. Alcoholism is a disease that is emotional, physical, and spiritual. It is not enough to arrest the physical part of the disease; an alcoholic without a recovery program is only a dry alcoholic.

If you are newly sober or drug-free, you should become involved in treatment and in programs such as Alcoholics Anonymous or Narcotics Anonymous in order to get a handle on your addiction. These programs address negative attitudes, emotions, and behaviors that interfere with staying sober. After one to two years of good sobriety, one may begin to work on one's codependency and adult-child issues in treatment or in ACOA. Getting in touch with "stuffed" feelings can threaten one's newly achieved sobriety. Substance abusers tend to use alcohol or drugs to either calm or numb themselves when they are upset. Thus the often painful feelings that may surface when dealing with adult-child issues could trigger drinking behavior for the newly sober.*

IV. SELF-HELP GROUPS FOR ADULT CHILDREN OF ALCOHOLICS—ACOA AND AL-ANON

A. *Exercise Two*
1. Objective: To increase members' awareness of self-help groups for adult children of alcoholics.
2. Discuss the following question as a group: Have you ever attended an ACOA meeting? If so, what was it like for you?

B. *Mini-Lecture: What Is ACOA?*
ACOA is a self-help group for men and women who were raised in alcoholic families. This fellowship of men and women share and work on common issues to increase personal awareness and growth. Through group support, acceptance, and validation, members diminish their sense of being alone with their problems and issues. Members share their experiences, strengths, and hopes with one another in an effort to solve their common problems and to help others recover from the effects of alcoholism. Like AA and Al-Anon, ACOA is a twelve-step program.

How does ACOA work? First, it reduces feelings of isolation. At meetings, the rules learned by adult children at an early age—don't talk, don't feel, don't trust—do not apply. You are encouraged to share your experiences, to talk about your issues and how you feel. Meetings provide a safe place where you can speak freely about yourselves and diminish your sense of isolation. The adult child begins to feel connected with other members in the group and to identify with what these people have to say, which breaks down his or her sense of isolation even further. It is a great relief to find out that you are not the only one who thinks or feels a certain way. It feels good to know that you are not crazy or bad, that your reactions and perceptions are normal or accurate. It feels wonderful to have your feelings or needs validated, perhaps for the first time in your life.

ACOA also breaks down your sense of isolation by providing a surrogate family. By attending meetings regularly, you will meet and get to know other people. For those of you who are not on good terms with your own families or whose families are not in a twelve-step program, the warmth and caring offered at meetings can mean a great deal. You are treated with respect, understanding, support, and compassion. You are accepted for who you are, however imperfect that may be.

ACOA builds self-esteem by providing members with the experience of being respected, accepted, and cared about. The feeling of being validated also increases self-esteem and reassures you that your feelings and perceptions are on target. When we feel others care about us, it increases our sense of self-worth and value.

ACOA promotes communication with others, which in turn breaks down some of the old barriers and increases trust. You learn that you can trust certain individuals with your feelings. Unlike your experience in an alcoholic home, what you say will not be used against you. You learn to trust yourself by learning to trust your instincts, perceptions, and feelings. The consistent support that individuals receive in ACOA enables them to make changes in their lives.

Adult children may want to work on personality issues, take a fearless and searching moral inventory, or work on character defects. The program provides a safe atmosphere for one to work on such issues. To work on a problem, one must first own that problem. Owning a problem becomes easier when you hear other people you like and respect publicly owning their problems at meetings. ACOA is a safe place to work on problems of character because individuals are not made to feel terrible for having or owning a problem, or for not being perfect. In fact, one is supported for acknowledging one's own problems. In the alcoholic home, it was a crime to be anything less than perfect; criticism was rarely constructive and often took the form of a personal attack.

For many, meetings may initially stir up painful feelings. It is not uncommon for individuals to feel depressed after their first few meetings. Some people may not return for a while. However, as one continues in the program, it becomes easier to face these feelings and old hurts.

ACOA focuses on the issues of the individual. The program emphasizes the importance of understanding how your past influences your present and continues to affect your daily life. However, the program emphasizes that you cannot use your history as an excuse for continuing your destructive behavior. Although the issues you have are the result of growing up in an alcoholic home, as an adult you are the only person who can work on changing how you deal with those issues. Recovery is up to you. Today as an adult, only you can be responsible for your happiness, recovery, and growth. Although you may be justifiably angry at your parents for what they did or did not do, you must understand that they, too, were victims of their own parents' behavior and of the disease of alcoholism.

Although ACOA is designed primarily for adult children of alcoholics, the preamble states that all are welcome. ACOA benefits any adult who grew up in a codependent family system in which emotional, physical, or sexual abuse might have occurred and in which parents tended to be rigid, to see things in black and white, and taught their children not to talk, feel, or trust. The adult child who is addicted to alcohol or drugs should not attend ACOA meetings until sobriety is achieved. If you are actively using alcohol or drugs, you cannot work on making any consistent changes in your life. It is recommended that one have at least one to one and a half years in AA before beginning to work on adult-child issues.*

ACOA meetings generally open with a reading of the problem, which consists of a list of adult-child issues. The problem may be followed by reading the solution:

The Solution: By attending Al-Anon and ACOA meetings on a regular basis we learn that we can live our lives in a more meaningful manner; we learn to change our attitudes and old patterns and habits to find serenity and even happiness.

- Alcoholism is a threefold disease—mental, physical, and spiritual. Our parents were victims of this disease, which ends in insanity, death, or, hopefully, recovery. Learning about and understanding the disease is the beginning of the gift of forgiveness.

- We learn the three Cs—we did not cause it, we cannot control it, and we cannot cure it.

- We learn to focus on ourselves and to be good to ourselves.

- We learn to detach with love and to give ourselves and others tough love.

- We use the Al-Anon slogans: "Let Go and Let God," "Easy Does It," "One Day at a Time," "Keep It Simple," "Live and Let Live." Using these slogans helps us lead our daily lives in a new way.

- We build our self-esteem by learning to feel our feelings, accept them, and express them.

- Through working the steps, we learn to accept the disease and realize that our lives have become unmanageable and that we are powerless over the disease and the alcoholic. As we admit our defects and our sick thinking, we are able to change our attitudes and to turn our reactions into actions. By working the program and admitting that we are powerless, we come to believe eventually in the spiritual aspects of the program. We learn that there is a solution other than ourselves—the group, a higher power, God as we understand Him. By sharing our experiences, relating to others, welcoming newcomers, and serving our group(s), we build self-esteem.

- We learn to love ourselves and others in a healthy way.

- We conduct telephone therapy with people whom we relate to, which is helpful at all times, not just when problems arise.

- By applying the Serenity Prayer to our daily lives, we begin to change the sick attitudes we acquired in childhood.

Following the reading of the Solution, the person who chairs the meeting picks an issue and relates his or her own experience regarding this issue. Following this, others share their experiences. Individuals have the option to pass. Meetings generally last one and a half hours. ACOA is supported through members' contributions for rental of a meeting place and coffee.

As mentioned earlier, ACOA is a self-help group based on the same twelve steps as AA and Al-Anon. As in these programs, spirituality is also emphasized. Some meetings open with the Serenity Prayer or close with the Lord's Prayer. Mention is sometimes made of turning things over or surrendering to one's higher power, be it God as one understands Him, or the program or group itself.

C. *Mini-Lecture: Is Al-Anon Helpful for Adult Children of Alcoholics?*
Al-Anon is also a helpful program for adult children of alcoholics, especially if they are in contact or still living with an alcoholic. Al-Anon is a self-help group for friends or family members of alcoholics. The program emphasizes that alcoholism is a family disease that affects each member emotionally, physically, and spiritually. The program educates family members that alcoholism is a disease that they cannot control and emphasizes that the only person who has control over his or her drinking is the alcoholic. Al-Anon helps indi-

viduals focus on themselves and encourages them to meet their own needs in a healthy way, rather than expending energy fruitlessly trying to control the alcoholic.

IV. Evaluation of the Workshop

A. *Closing Discussion and Termination*
   1. Give members an opportunity to review and share their experience in the group.
   2. Ask members if they found it difficult to talk about certain topics.
   3. Thank members for participating and attending.
   4. Ask members what they found most valuable or most helpful.
   5. Pass out list of names and phone numbers of those members who wish to share this information.
   6. Encourage members to continue in ACOA, especially if they found this eight-week seminar helpful.
   7. If group members feel the need to work further on adult children of alcoholics issues, suggest that they consider either individual or group therapy.

B. *Evaluation*
   Ask group to complete a written evaluation form (see handout). The evaluation gives group members a chance to examine the effects of the workshop on themselves and to evaluate the content and process of the group.

REFERENCES

1. Janet Geringer Woititz, *Adult Children of Alcoholics* (Pompano Beach, Fla.: Health Communications, 1983), pp. 52–56, 92–96.

HANDOUT—SESSION 8

We would appreciate your help in evaluating this group.

A. Listed below are subject areas that were covered in the eight sessions. Please mark each of these with one of the following responses:

> 1—Most Helpful
> 2—Somewhat Helpful
> 3—Least Helpful

_____ How the child is affected by the alcoholic parent's inconsistent behavior.

_____ How the alcoholic home is not conducive to developing self-esteem

_____ How one is affected by the rules of the home

_____ Don't talk

_____ Don't feel

_____ Don't trust

_____ Why adult children feel isolated and afraid of people

_____ Understanding one's feelings of guilt, hurt, anger, sadness, and fear

_____ Why adult children tend to "stuff" their feelings

_____ Why one must learn to express one's feelings

_____ The roles in the alcoholic home that were played out as a child and now as an adult

_____ Why adult children are set up to depend on alcoholism

_____ What kinds of relationships adult children gravitate toward

_____ Overreacting to changes over which one has no control

_____ Difficulty dealing with conflict

_____ Addiction to excitement

_____ Fear of abandonment

_____ Issues surrounding loyalty

_____ Difficulty in intimate relationships

_____ Guidelines for a healthy intimate relationship

_____ Difficulty with impulsive behavior

_____ Resources for help

B. Please indicate how helpful you found the following:

> 1—Most Helpful
> 2—Somewhat Helpful
> 3—Least Helpful

_____ Information provided by leader
_____ Meeting other people with common concerns
_____ Working in small groups
_____ Large group discussion of specific topics
_____ Handouts

C. Please answer the following questions:

Yes No

☐ ☐ There was a proper balance between lectures and discussion.

☐ ☐ Overall, I found the workshop helpful.

☐ ☐ There was a proper balance between group discussion and working in twos.

☐ ☐ This workshop helped increase both my intellectual and emotional awareness as an adult child of an alcoholic.

☐ ☐ This workshop made me aware of my options for recovery.

☐ ☐ Would you be interested in participating in a therapy group for adult children of alcoholics here at our agency?